ON TRYING TO TEACH

The Mind in Correspondence

M. Robert Gardner

THE ANALYTIC PRESS

1994   Hillsdale, NJ   London

Published by The Analytic Press, Inc.
101 West Street, Hillsdale, NJ 07642

First paperback printing 1997

Typeset by TechType Inc., Upper Saddle River, NJ

Library of Congress Cataloguing-in-Publication Data

Gardner, M. Robert
        On trying to teach : the mind in correspondence / M.
        Robert Gardner
        p. cm.
        ISBN   0-88163-281-3
        1. Teaching 2. Teaching—Psychological aspects. 3.
        Teachers. 4. Teacher-student relationships. I. Title
LB1025.3.G37   1994
271.1'02—dc20   94-28731
                                                            CIP

Printed in the United States of America
10 9 8 7 6 5 4 3 2 1

"Self is the sole subject we study and learn . . . I bring myself to sea, to Malta, to Italy, to find new affinities between myself and my fellowmen, to observe narrowly the affections, weaknesses, surprises, hopes, doubts, which new sides of the panorama shall call forth in me."

Ralph Waldo Emerson, *Letters*

Contents

BOOK II
A GENTLE SYMBIOSIS
The Student and the Teacher

On Essaying Teaching

A teacher is a peculiar person. A teacher of psychoanalysis is particularly peculiar; not content to practice one impossible profession, he or she practices two. A teacher of psychoanalysis with the gall to write about teaching displays peculiarities and courts impossibilities too staggering to contemplate. Still, that's what I have decided to do. Or that's what I feel compelled to do.

I did not set out to write a book about teaching. I set out to keep a journal. I favor journal-keeping that starts with nothing in particular and turns out to be about something in particular. The entries from which these essays were gleaned turned out to be about teaching.

Some parts of this book follow a linear logic. Others conspicuously do not. I have tried to highlight a few stubbornly recurrent themes while preserving the evidence that the work as a whole is a palimpsest. I have tried also to highlight the way, as the mind wanders, almost-but-not-quite-acknowledged questions appear, disappear, and re-appear in one figure and another in unending, if unsteady, spirals.

Those who know teachers will know that teachers know remarkably little about learning and teaching; which remarkable ignorance makes it extremely hard for a teacher to write anything about teaching without telling others how to teach. I have tried to control that telling temptation and to stick to describing the dilemmas and challenges I have faced in teaching, in thinking about teaching, and in working toward a philosophy and way of teaching. Book I is about those dilemmas and challenges. Book II is about an approach I have found useful—sometimes useful—in facing them. No persons who are teachers by profession, and no parents, politicians, or any others who find occasion to teach without professing to be teachers, and no persons who have been or are being taught by persons who either profess or do not, are forbidden to read either part.

E. B. White once said that an essayist is a self-liberated man sustained by the childish belief that everything that happens to him is of general interest. Only a person who is congenitally self-centered, he opined, has the effrontery and stamina to write essays.

In my view, E.B., as an essayist, is tops. In his theory of character, however, I believe he had it all wrong. Persons compelled to write essays have very little of the sturdy confidence he suggests. To the contrary, unsure of themselves and their visions, they need to set down the most trivial of their experiences in order to take—or get—a fix. Nor do they, as E.B. suggests, assume what they say will be of interest to others. Those who write essays write only to imaginary companions. If some of those companions become real, and if some of them find something of interest in those essays, these serendipitous developments come as a delightful surprise.

Beginnings

At sixteen, inspired by an intemperate idealism and an enthusiastic high school advisor, I set off for far-off Brownsville where at the close of several school days a week I tried to teach remedial English to a dozen or more unenthusiastic students who had flunked their previous studies. Though my destination was Brownsville, Brooklyn, not Brownsville, Texas, it might have been the latter for all I knew of the former. Moreover, though my students had optimistically been designated as requiring remedial work, their dilemmas and my own might better have been acknowledged by designating the enterprise an effort to learn and to teach English as a second language. Whatever its right name, the project was not conspicuously successful.

A dozen years later, I did teach in Texas in circumstances not entirely different from those I had experienced farther north. One of my duties as an Air Force psychiatrist was to instruct unenthusiastic corpsmen in the art of interviewing unhappy recruits to speed their timely return to the communities from which they had been untimely ripped. In those days, recruiters were paid a bounty for each recruit; the numbers, therefore, if not the capabilities of the recruits, were impressive. Nevertheless, despite the large service we rendered to the Air Force and the nation by sending those recruits swiftly home, and despite my best efforts to stir a fitting interest in the development of the skills needed to expedite those home-sendings, few corpsmen whom I had the privilege of teaching showed as much interest in performing those patriotic activities as in producing gin in the still they had built in a back room of our not very military clinic.

Not long after the completion of those exercises in pedagogy, on return to the Boston Psychopathic Hospital, I was judged ready to teach the rudiments of psychiatry, psychotherapy, and psychoanalytic psychology to medical students, psychiatric residents, nurses, chaplains, social workers, psychologists, sociologists, and others whose credentials I never learned. With an eagerness born more of ignorance than a grasp of the scope of the task, I accepted the assignment, met repeatedly with those persons in large groups and small, and subjected them to lectures, seminars, clinical demonstrations, tutorials, and supervision.

I believe these early experiences played a large part in stirring my subsequent wonderings about how best to teach students of whose interests, skills, and needs I have often found myself ignorant. And these wonderings quickened when shortly after the completion of my analytic schooling I found myself teaching psychoanalytic theory to classes of thirty or more analytic students. Over several years, I prepared carefully, polished persistently, and delivered uneasily a series of lectures on what was designated officially as instinct theory and ego psychology. As a consequence of that now familiar unfamiliarity with my students, to say nothing of my questionable qualifications for teaching the particulars I was trying to teach, I found myself wrestling often with vexing questions about the value, if any, of my teachings to my students. In assessing that value, I had the boon and burden of many chances to observe the later development of many of these students and to hear some of their views on what they had and had not learned.

These experiences, augmented by later opportunities to observe some ways in which some learning unfolds in the microcosm of one-on-one teaching, have aided and abetted my long struggle to find a better fit between what my students want and are ready to learn and what I want and am ready to teach. In teaching I have often been reminded of what Marshall said is the job of a general: "to make important decisions on the basis of inadequate information." This book contains a few reflections and ramifications of such efforts.

BOOK I

THE SCHOOL OF SOFT KNOCKS

The Furor to Teach

"The true teacher defends his pupil against his own influence."
A. Bronson Alcott, *Orphic Sayings*

1

A. Bronson Alcott was the idealist's idealist. True to his persuasion, he failed to mention in that Orphic saying that for the true teacher to "defend his pupil against his own influence" is a very tough task. The struggle to attain the recommended defense must take place, if it can, in the face of the true teacher's defining affliction: the furor to teach.

What's a furor to teach? It's a menace. It's a menace to teachers, to students, and to innocent bystanders. Teachers possessed by that furor are in trouble. Teachers devoid of that furor—if such can be called teachers—are in more trouble. Teachers are damned if they have it and damned if they don't.

To temper furor to itch, to make it less a menace and more a grace, a teacher needs a highly refined sense of dispensability. Becoming a teacher is like becoming president. No one should be given the job who wants it too much.

But where can anyone be found with both the required furor and the required restraint? Who but a person badly bit by the teaching bug would put up with the conditions of teaching? And of the persons so bitten, who could manage, and by what means, to temper the furor to teach?

Come hell or high water, the true teacher will teach, and will do so whether that teaching makes sense or not. Offer the best conditions, attract the most reasonable persons, warn them carefully of the terrible risks; yet the many problems of furor-full teaching will stubbornly persist. The cap of a teacher readily becomes the cap of a dunce.

Appoint any energetic man or woman to the teacher's job and in short order that teacher will regard indispensable whatever he or she chooses to teach and whatever method by which he or she chooses to teach it. The true teacher will always find something that needs to be taught, the method by which it needs to be taught, and the person who needs to be taught what that teacher regards necessary to teach by that necessary method.

The true teacher never rests. Every happening reminds the true teacher of a story; every story needs telling. Show the true teacher an apple seed and, unlike Johnny Appleseed, the true teacher is never content to plant a tree. The true teacher will not stop till he or she can find a person upon whom to inflict a history of the uses of the apple in the Western world along with an extended exegesis of the symbolism of the apple from the Old Testament to the present. And given the slightest chance, without a smidgen of concern for the effects of these pedagogical charges on the victims, the true teacher will toss in a dissertation on the differences between the apple and the pomegranate. What's more, the true teacher's transgressions are customarily made more terrible by speedy transmogrification into noble ends. And once that ennoblement has taken place, the true teacher, pursuing those noble ends, shows little mercy or restraint and not a trace of redemptive shame.

It's a safe bet it was not Aesop but a true teacher, or perhaps a committee of true teachers, who put those silly lessons at the foot of Aesop's fables. Who else would tack on to such lively tales such pale abstractions and tiresome truisms? And who else but a true teacher would reveal so little concern for the dangerous consequences of telling so many cautionary tales?

The true teacher, especially in those packs called schools, with a flair that comes of a mix of inborn talent and rigorous practice, displays a canny knack of selecting the most exciting experiences and transforming them magically into the most insipid. A true teacher's work is never done.

A. Bronson Alcott said, "The true teacher defends his student against his own influence." He meant it would be nice if we could.

2

With little or no provocation, I have quoted Alcott's saying to many true teachers; of those, many have surmised that Alcott meant the true teacher should defend the student against the student's own influence. I take this understandable, if deplorable, misunderstanding as incontrovertible evidence of the virulence of the furor to teach.

Of those few true teachers who have grasped that Alcott meant that the true teacher should guard the student against the true teacher's own influence, few have known how. And, of those, still fewer proved eager to perform that guardian function. True teachers want too much to teach, want to teach too much, and want too much to teach what they want to teach whenever, however, and to whomever they want.

The true teacher's furor to teach rivals in its intensity, and in the havoc it wreaks, the physician's furor to cure. And like true physicians, true teachers sometimes know the disorder but seldom the cure.

In principle, true teachers rarely fail to appreciate moderation, tact, timing, and other agreeable practices. But principles go out the window when, convinced they possess indispensable knowledge, true teachers are driven to dispense it.

Without the furor to teach, true teachers are most unlikely to move themselves or their students. But the line between helpful furor and harmful is full of lost edges and, consequently, of lost teachers and students. Beset by so many furors to teach and finding so many students so ignorant of what they feel compelled to teach, true teachers, despite their grand respect for the human mind—if not for many particular minds—often find their students' minds to be vacuums, which, since like Nature, true teachers abhor, they feel compelled to fill. Moreover, when students rebuff their efforts to impart the necessary wisdom, rebuffed true teachers are moved to higher and higher levels of furor; furor begets opposition begets furor begets opposition and on and on. The consequent concatenations—explosive bursts within an orderly progression—show a beauty and stability that rival Bach's Pasacaglia in C Minor, and, not infrequently, Krebb's cycle.

Recently, a friend and true teacher told me of an instance. Well along in a course meant to stir students to open their minds to ideas and customs customarily regarded foreign, a student denounced the piece of American Indian music then under consideration. He declared the music primitive. He clearly meant "not good." He said the music was repetitive and the persons who made it had not changed their music, themselves, or anything else for thousands of years. Not content with that, he went on to compare those backward persons to others he had visited in a far off nation and had found sitting around all day doing nothing but making music, and primitive music at that.

My friend, ever the true teacher, tried to invite further consideration of what the student regarded primitive and what he regarded progressive. That invitation met with minimal success. Another student chimed in with several pithy remarks about my friend's peculiar musical and literary tastes. He said those tastes might be acceptable in the university from which he knew his teacher had come, but he found them weird. He added several references to foreigners, university and other, who carry on in rites no right-thinking person would or should take seriously.

Pity my poor friend. His students and he are well along in a course planned to promote thoughtful consideration of what at first may seem foreign. And now he is faced with attitudes and acts that make him wonder how he could have tried so hard and taught so little. Moreover, in this lively moment, adding injury to insult, prejudices against the foreign have switched location. They are no longer abstractions about persons remote in time and space; the deplorable foreigner is now the teacher himself. And the two outspoken students, who probably speak bravely, if not wisely, for others, find the teacher's foreign tastes doubly misguided: pretentious in form and primitive in substance.

Unable at last to stand such primitive thinking about primitive thinking, my friend, the true teacher, challenged forthrightly the premise that progress should necessarily be measured by the standards of the Industrial Revolution and that primitive should necessarily be defined as the failure to live up to those standards. He got nowhere with that. He got nowhere with several other praiseworthy sentiments. At last, my exasperated friend asked the more vociferous of the students whether a recent shocking happening in that student's own neck of the woods was not at least as primitive as the happenings the student had so strongly deplored.

A true teacher never quits. Unfortunately, however, on this occasion no discernible progress was made toward defining the nature of progress or even toward advancing questions of what is civilized progress and primitive stagnation, or what is primitive progress and civilized stagnation. It's unclear what the students learned. My friend learned that his urge to teach an open-minded view toward the "foreign" had led him to demonstrate a closed-minded view toward his students' foreign views on foreign views.

I have not reported these events to play Monday-morning quarterback. Nor do I suggest that this teaching effort was without merit or that the teacher should have practiced the unwavering relativism some teachers practice and more are accused of. All true teachers know that meeting provocation with provocation often proves unavoidable and occasionally useful. I want only to highlight in the aforementioned academic exchange a common quandary of all true teachers: in the grip of our furors to teach, we not infrequently display in our very ways of teaching the very opposite of what we set out so reasonably and resolutely to teach.

3

Each furor to teach is goaded and guided by each teacher's theory of what is essential to teach. And each furor is heightened by conditions specific to the teacher's character, persuasion, and current preoccupations. The true teacher, however, of whatever character, persuasion, or preoccupation, finds it particularly hard to temper the furor to teach when confronted with a student whom that teacher judges in urgent need of learning what that teacher is in urgent need of teaching. And temperance is made still more difficult when that teacher judges that what the student needs to learn is something the student should have been taught long ago. Little can fan the furor to teach more furiously than the true teacher's perception that time is running out. The true teacher works on a very tight schedule.

"How can a student have come so far and not learned to spell?" we ask. "How can a student not know by now the third law of thermodynamics?" We marvel at what our students have failed to learn from us. We marvel even more at what our students have failed to learn from others. We are admirably alert to the everpresent need for radical reforms of the systems of teaching by which other teachers prepare their students for our teaching.

Forced frequently to teach what others should already

have taught, we are driven by that unpleasant necessity to teach immoderately. Finding ourselves occasionally with sufficient time and opportunity to teach what we want especially to teach, we are driven by that pleasant possibility also to teach immoderately. Obligation and opportunity are partners, though rarely equal, in our furors to teach.

When teaching, as much as we are moved by despair, we are moved by hope. Faced with an unusually promising or unpromising student—and to the true teacher, all students are unusually promising or unpromising—we feel inspired to pass along any and all information that might someday count. Accordingly, the true teacher often resembles the old minor league catcher in *Bull Durham* who, in preparing the rookie on his way to the "show" advises; "You gotta learn your cliches."

When I first became a teacher, and long after, whether teaching students I regarded unusually promising or unpromising, I taught often as young children teach their youngers. That is, I taught enthusiastically what I needed to teach to boost my belief in what I had learned lately and digested, assimilated, or eliminated insufficiently. To that end, I taught the wisdom of my elders to my youngers in doctrines far holier than those of the elders by whom I had lately been taught.

In time, I corrected that error. With the passage of more time, I corrected that correction till at last, deploring my field's decline, I was driven once again by the furor to teach, this time driven to convey the wisdom of yesterday to the philistines of today. A true teacher travels in circles and hopes they are, if looked at from the right angle, upward spirals.

I have found myself subject to the fullest furors to teach when consumed by the notion that I know something—something inherited or newly discovered—that my students not only need urgently to learn but are able to learn only from me. I can hardly ever resist that double charge of singular necessity and sole possibility. Convinced I'm at the cutting edge of my field, mixing metaphor and paradox, I cling tenaciously to the belief that I am the port of last call.

My task has not been made easier by my being a clinical teacher. When life and death matters are at stake, and to the true clinician they often seem to be, I end up in the most awful predicaments. Though eager for my students to learn in their own best sequences and paces, nevertheless, when a patient's health is at risk, and it often seems to be, I cannot help telling precipitously what my students must and must not do. In which event, I have been known to dispense such information in ways about as useful—as Freud said of the intemperate dispensing of "deep" interpretations—as handing out menus in time of famine.

And when I am sat-in-upon and watched by examiners, I'm worse. Feeling pressed to show what I can teach, I'm moved even more than ordinarily to overteach. Which, given my ordinary furor to teach, I don't need. I have therefore come to the view that the time-honored method of testing true teachers by sitting in on them and watching is best for showing them at their worst and worst for showing them at their best. The watched teacher is quickest to boil.

In any case, I have come to the general conclusion that, watched or not, true teachers are driven by an irresponsible responsibility to see paints used properly, musical notes played properly, low fastballs swung at properly, sentences constructed properly, scientific canons followed properly, skis pointed and edged properly, patients treated properly, and much else. Whatever our arts and sciences, we teach with high furor the proper pursuit of that art or science; to that end, we try often to teach the unteachable or to teach the teachable in ways unmanageable.

A. Bronson Alcott says, "The true teacher defends his pupil against his own influence." Unfortunately for true teachers, however, and for the students of true teachers, A. Bronson Alcott, perhaps trying to defend us against his own influence, doesn't tell how.

The Unknown Student

*"It is not often that any man can have so much knowledge of
another as is necessary to make instruction useful."*
Samuel Johnson, *The Rambler* 87

1

Despite Johnson's warning, Joaquim Sorolla y Bastida once
said to everyone in general and so to no one of whom he was
likely to have had much knowledge, "Art has no business
dealing with anything ugly or sad."

Some critics find Sorolla's claim sadly mistaken. Others
find it fatuous, arrogant, or otherwise disagreeable. Few critics,
however, are likely to be surprised to see a teacher of such
distinction leaping so grandly and falling so flat on his face. It's
precisely the willingness—the eagerness—to dare such grand
rises and falls that makes a teacher a true teacher.

If Sorolla needs any additional defense, it can be said without reservation that whatever his shortcomings of preaching and painting, he was in his painting true to his preaching. Nearly always eschewing the ugly and the sad, he skillfully painted thousands of spirited pictures of the Spanish sunlight falling on one sparkling surface and another, and so, nearly always living up to his sanguine aims, he gained his deservedly enduring reputation as the Spanish Sargent.

But even those critics most inclined to give Sorolla passing grades for his consistency rarely grade him as charitably for his insistence that "Art has no business dealing with anything ugly or sad." If Sorolla had been content to say he painted best when he painted what he found beautiful and cheery, if he had said that sunny scenes filled him with an exuberant urge to paint, if he had said that the ugly and the sad stifled his painterly spirits, these affirmations would have formed a portrait of a different color. What's more, it seems unlikely that any critics would have raised a ruckus or an eyebrow if Sorolla had said he preferred to paint the flamingo or the flamenco.

If Sorolla had spoken in a more self-confining and accordingly more self-defining voice, if he had simply said 'Here's how I find I paint best; how do you find you paint best?,' if he had shown any appreciation that his preferences had been shaped by the fashions of his day, his history, geography, biology, temperament, skills, and much else, it seems likely that most critics who have found his actual pronouncement grossly unacceptable would join Sorolla willingly in joyful consideration of the conditions that make a painter paint what and how that painter paints. If Sorolla had only spoken of what he preferred to do rather than of what others must do, which of all his critics would insist that he paint the ugly and the sad?

And if Sorolla had spoken in a different voice, which of his harshest critics, knowing that when he was two he lost his mother and father in a cholera epidemic, would fail to be touched by his steadfast determination to avoid the ugly and the sad? For that matter, knowing of the same tragic events, who would lack sympathy if Sorolla had asserted he preferred, or felt obliged, to paint only the ugly and the sad?

But when Sorolla proclaims that all Art should be confined to what he chooses – and may have no choice but – to paint, few critics are sympathetic. And many are downright vexed by his speaking of "Art" with a capital A and of his own view of art as if it the be all and end all. Indeed, if he had proclaimed to one of my teachers that "Art has no business dealing with anything ugly or sad," Sorolla would have been likely to hear in reply, "Who is it, Señor, whom you call Art?"

I don't know if Sorolla knew Samuel Johnson. Given Johnson's provincial hankering for London, Sorolla's and Johnson's paths may never have crossed. Probably Sorolla did not know Johnson. But even if he knew him, Sorolla seems not to have known enough to heed Johnson's warning: "It is not often that any man can have so much knowledge of another as is necessary to make instruction useful." With no knowledge of the nature, needs, opinions, interests, fascinations, capacities, strengths, weaknesses, dilemmas, quandaries, perplexities, challenges, and other circumstances of those he was trying to teach, Sorolla did not shrink from telling all painters what they should and should not paint nor from telling all painters and nonpainters what paintings they should and should not take seriously.

Critics have tried to explain Sorolla's craving for the pontifical on the grounds of character. They say his talk was always filled with "should," "must," "no business with," "always," "never," "everything," "nothing," and "the only way to." They say that even in the most casual conversation Sorolla persistently converted his preferences into principles. I have even seen it recorded that Sorolla repeatedly urged each of his three children to become painters because "painting is the only way to be happy in life."

But such slurs on Sorolla's character miss the point. Sorolla was a teacher. It's a teacher's job to convert preferences into principles.

It's easy to scoff at Sorolla. It's easy to scoff at all teachers. But consider the teacher's dilemma. Finding that some of our best teaching comes of finding something about ourselves that is somewhat true of others, we are encouraged to the pronun-

ciamentos we are anyway eager to make. It's easy to say that
Sorolla knew too little about the students he wished to teach
and about himself.

Such Sorolla-bashing, however, ignores the climate in
which true teachers teach. Driven by our furors to teach, we
have little leaning for learning about the persons we hope to
teach or about ourselves and our idiosyncratic ways of teaching. Which ignorance puts us more at the mercy of our furors
to teach. Which decreases our already lagging sensitivity to the
conditions of those persons we hope to teach.

It may be all well and good for Johnson to say, with
Boswell at heel, "It's not often that any man can have so much
knowledge of another as is necessary to make instruction
useful." But did Johnson follow his own instruction?

And how can a teacher "have so much knowledge of
another as is necessary to make instruction useful"? True
teachers swing on high limbs. Failing to move from the
personal to the universal, we bore. Leaping lightly from the
personal to the universal, we fall; and falling, we leave our
mark on disciples who, in empty compliance, paint only the
pretty and the happy, or on dissidents, who, in empty defi-
ance, paint only the ugly and the sad.

2

I'm always on the lookout for writing tips, particularly from
writers who swing a mean pen. In a Sunday book section of
The New York Times, I once found an especially promising tip
by Annie Dillard. She suggested that would-be writers would
be more likely to put first things first if, while writing, they
imagined themselves to be dying.

Occasionally while writing I have had a sense of dying.
But it never occurred to me to take the extra step of seeking that
sense. Nevertheless, having long felt a lively affection for
Uncas, Chopin, Camille, Mimi, and others of that nobly fading
ilk, I found Dillard's suggestion arresting. And I could readily

appreciate how the urgent demands of that unhappy moment—speak now or forever hold your piece—would help me to forsake the trivial and cleave to the essential. If I could but imagine myself dying—and so have little to lose but life— I would dare to speak the large unspoken truths I have long yearned, but failed, to speak.

The prospect of being focused on the alpha and the omega and of putting them speedily and bluntly into words—what would-be writer does not dream of writing first drafts that are last?—was downright uplifting. In addition, I anticipated the gain of being able once and for all to stop shuffling about in the lengthy and demanding preparations with which I customarily prepare for and postpone writing.

Dillard did not stop with the recommendation of my demise. She advised me to imagine myself not only a dying writer but a dying writer writing to dying readers. Perhaps you can imagine the intellectual appeal of her advice, but I doubt you can imagine the glee with which I greeted her plan for overcoming in one funereal swoop my proclivities to procrastinate, to belabor the insignificant, and to write in pusillanimous voice. If as a dying writer I failed to write quickly, wisely, and bluntly for my own expiring sake, how could I fail to do so for the sake of my day-numbered reader?

I regret to report, however, that this ingenious and lively experiment in coterminous termination produced in my case minimal communicative generation. Though I gave Dillard's double terminal method my best shot, it did not work. It did not even almost work. But I'll say this: I have long admired Dillard's writing; now I admire it more. To anyone who can write under the conditions she proposes, I tip my hat.

Perhaps I should have known right off that Dillard's teaching could not improve my writing. If I cannot paint as Sorolla tells me, why should I think I can write as Dillard tells me? That's obvious from afar. Close up, however, I have always found it hard to maintain a proper cynicism when a teacher of obvious talent suggests a way to transform the difficult into the simple.

Dillard might claim I failed to give her method a fair shot. But that's not so. Though it's hard when you're feeling frisky to imagine yourself in extremis, I managed repeatedly to get into a highly credible about-to-expire mood; moreover, I did not choose to take the easy way out— to go West (or South) all at once—but rather to fade away slowly as heroes and heroines do in the very best operas, plays, movies, novels, and poems; which largo departures make sense to me, since in the throes of a more immediate demise, how could anyone manage to finish an aria, speech, book, villain, or much else, before he or she were finished?

Nevertheless, when I imagined my reader and me on our joint ways out, sorrow made my tears considerably more copious than my words. And even when I had recovered enough to write down my thoughts, I was driven so strongly to come up with a bit of deathless prose that in search of that last grasp at immortality I couldn't find anything that qualified as a good-enough last-gasp testimony.

There's no getting around it. I'm not in Annie Dillard's league. I don't have it in me to be a world-class moribund writer. If I were the dying Caesar, I would never manage anything so erudite and elegant as the bilingual "Et tu, Brute? Then die, Caesar." When the chips are down, even the prosaic "Morituri te salutamus" would be far beyond my means.

Let's face it. It's my nature to react morbidly to the slightest signs of my mortality. Expressive final exits are not my metier. Outward bound, I lack the amazing grace. I'm not even good at ordinary good-byes. I'm more likely to come up with "So long kid," than "Parting is such sweet sorrow." Some persons grow eloquent when bidding farewell. I grow trite or mute. More my way than a final productivity is a terminal taciturnity or triviality.

Dillard knew none of that about me. Nor did she know or bother to learn that I'm much older than she. If at her age she can feign a well-documented exit, good for her; but let's see her do it at mine. And she didn't know that even when I'm not pretending to be a dying writer writing to a dying reader, I'm already overburdened by an overreaching for immortality. I don't need a written invitation to write for the ages. And yet, unaware of my condition, Dillard did not hesitate to advise me to imagine myself a dying writer writing to a dying reader.

On balance, I found Dillard's life-cutting short-cut to concise writing about as useful as putting a microphone in someone's hands and inviting that person, in the few seconds before the commercial break, to say something pithy and majestic to millions of eager listeners. Dillard was not at her best when she tried to teach me to write. How she manages to carry on so admirably as a dying writer writing to a dying reader, I have not the foggiest notion. She also failed to teach me that.

I'm sure Dillard would have done better to advise me to imagine having all the time in the world to write to readers with all the time in the world: immortal to immortal, so to speak. Still, Dillard helped me to remember that what makes one writer feel at home makes another feel abroad. A writer once told me he could write only using yellow legal size pads and a well-sharpened number two pencil. I have learned that my own writing goes better when my sleep goes poorly. That is, my writing goes better when, having thought long by day about what I want to write, I hover long by night between asleep and awake till I awake in the morning with something ready to be writ. If I were a writer, and a teacher of writing, would it therefore be good for me to announce that the secret of writing lies in seeking insomnia?

Joaquim Sorolla y Bastida failed to help me to paint. Annie Dillard failed to help me to write. And I cannot help wondering what would have happened to Joaquim Sorolla y Bastida if, applying Annie Dillard's doleful advice to his painting, he had gone against his heart-felt conviction that Art has no business with the ugly or the sad and had tried instead to imagine himself a dying painter painting for a dying viewer. Or, for that matter, suppose Annie Dillard, despite her grand and morbid preference for the decidedly mournful, were to take Joaquim Sorolla y Bastida's chipper advice and confine herself to the happy and the pretty. I imagine that in each instance the sad and ugly consequences would give pause to any would-be teacher.

Such contemplation has heightened my appreciation of Samuel Johnson's observation, "It is not often that any man can have so much knowledge of another as is necessary to make instruction useful." And I am grateful for his valuable instruction about the hazards of uninformed instruction. I cannot figure out, however, how he gained so much knowledge of me as is necessary to make his instruction useful.

Gulliver at Home and Abroad

> "We are not quite at our ease in the presence of a schoolmaster
> because we are conscious he is not quite at his ease in ours. He
> is awkward and out of place in the society of his equals. He
> comes like Gulliver from his little people and he cannot fit the
> stature of his understanding to yours."
> Charles Lamb, *The Old and The New Schoolmaster*.

A few years ago, the president of a large New England
university announced his intention to run for nomination as his
party's candidate for governor of his state. He began his
campaign with several highly questionable remarks about
immigrants, welfare, and alcoholism. Many outraged citizens
responded. Among them was an alumna of the university of
which the would-be governor was president. In her letter to a
local newspaper, she quoted Virginia Woolf (Orlando):

"The intellect, divine as it is, and all worshipful, has a
habit of lodging in the most seedy of carcasses, and
often, alas, acts the cannibal among the other faculties
so that often, where the Mind is the biggest, the Heart,
the Senses, Magnanimity, Charity, Tolerance, Kindliness, and the rest of them scarcely have room to
breathe."

Subsequently, several readers hailed the perspicacity of
Virginia Woolf and of the letterwriter who quoted her remark.
One reader cheered the deftness with which the teacher-
candidate was hoist by his academic petard. Another found it
especially fit that his comeuppance had been delivered by a
graduate of his own institution.

I was of mixed mind. I was pleased that the ugly biases of
the university president who aspired to be governor had been
met with the appropriate opprobrium. But I was also of the
view that anyone willing for the common good to accept a
demotion from president to governor could not be all bad.

To this day I suspect that if any graduate of any institution
of learning shows, as this letterwriter did, such conspicuous
independence and impressive acumen, the president of that
institution is unlikely to be as thoroughly or consistently bad as
his public pronouncements and his critics have made him
appear. And though this particular offending university president may deserve little or no credit for the virtues of this
alumna, and still less for his highly offensive remarks, I believe
that anyone who has toiled long in the deplorable vineyards in
which such outlandish perspectives are likely to take root
deserves considerably more sympathy than this poor fellow
received.

I don't dispute the accuracy of Virginia Woolf's observations regarding the consequences of an intellect run wild. Nor
do I dispute the alumna's astute grasp of the relevance of
Woolf's observations to the deplorable attitudes of the president of her erstwhile university. I rejoice in Woolf's and the
alumna's sharpness of eye, ear, and tongue. But I wish they

had shown a touch of compassion for those who labor in an atmosphere poisoned by ivory.

I don't claim it would be good to make this or any other college president, or teacher, governor. I hold no neo-Platonist brief for scholars trying to become governors, senators, or presidents. (Look what happened with Woodrow Wilson.) But I say we should try to understand the disorders of teachers and try to treat teachers with the same sympathy and respect we usually extend to disordered others, especially those whose disorders are service connected.

Some skeptics might assert that the aforementioned ailments of the aforementioned university president were not service connected since the teacher was always so afflicted, or at least always so predisposed. They might say the same of all teachers. But that's unfair. In any line of work, if we have any choice, we seek the circumstances in which we can express our predispositions. If we then get what we deserve, are we any less deserving of compassion? What, then, is the point of Greek tragedy?

What we teachers would like widely understood is that the conditions in which we work, the conditions in which we choose bravely to work, are unusually hazardous. We are sick of being thought to lead a soft life. Nothing is further from the truth.

Who but the most courageous, the most public-spirited, and the most self-sacrificing persons would choose an occupation that places them at the mercy of their furors to teach, exposes them to the hazards of trying to teach persons they barely know, and encourages them—expects them—to indulge repeatedly in the most hazardous exercises of the intellect? Is there a person who can long pursue a career of teaching without succumbing to the terrible temptation to play captain on the bridge, Connecticut Yankee in King Arthur's court, Moses, divus, or diva, or without otherwise being engulfed in complex Gulliver complexes? Is it any surprise that a university president develops the peculiar notion that he is suited to be governor? Is it not more a surprise, if it is true, that he aspires no higher? Is it any surprise that he is out of touch with life lived outside his University? Is it not more a surprise that he is not more out of touch? Breathes there a teacher who can long breathe classroom air without suffering the terrible consequences Virginia Woolf accurately if unsympathetically named: suffocation of Heart, Senses, Magnanimity, Charity, Tolerance, and Kindliness?

Criticize teachers, yes; but give the poor devils their work compensatory due.

On Teacherly Versatility

A teacher who applied for a job in a small rural school was asked: "How will you teach the creation of man?" Knowing his answer might prove unacceptable, but unable to discern what was wanted, he was dismayed. After a moment, however, his face lit up. He replied: "I can teach it either way."

Anonymous

Teaching "either way" is one way teachers display their versatility in the face of informational insufficiency. My clock radio reminded me of this way and more.

I keep my clock radio tuned to an educational network. Educational networks are sometimes called public networks to conceal their true purpose. But whatever called, educational networks put many listeners to sleep. Mine wakes me up.

The other day, I awoke to a program called "Ask Dr.

Science." The caller asked, "Why can you never find a cop when you need one?"

Dr. Science replied, "One might ask, Why do you always look for a cop when there's none around?"

At first, I thought this a parody on psychoanalysts. But soon, with the help of an enlightening shower, I remembered that answering questions with questions is not the invention of psychoanalysts. They have tinkered with the tool for but a hundred years. Teachers invented it.

The basic ways of answering questions with questions were invented by teachers in Mesopotamia about two thousand years B.C. Since then, teachers have advanced other ways of turning things around to fit the view from on high till, by the end of the twentieth century, all true teachers, when questioned about matters of which they know little or nothing, can readily turn the asker's attention to another question and can do so with consummate ease. The modern true teacher, therefore, when confronted by even the most complex question, is never dismayed and seldom puzzled.

Take Dr. Science. Knowing little or nothing about the problems about which the caller asks, Dr. Science invites the caller to turn attention from the problems of outer streets to those of inner. And Dr. Science executes this turnabout with exquisite tact. He does not say the caller's attention must or should be directed inward. He says it might. "One might ask . . ." he says. Who can argue with that? Conditionals are among a true teacher's strongest operationals.

And just as Dr. Science doesn't insist that his question be asked, he doesn't insist that his question be answered and doesn't even claim ownership of the question. He doesn't say, as a less experienced person might, "My question is . . ." or "I wonder why . . ." He doesn't say, "I want to ask . . ." He doesn't ask, "Why do you . . . ?" He merely says offhandedly, "*One* might ask . . ." Dr. Science skillfully sets his question adrift in a lofty atmosphere to which he happens to have informed access. He crowds neither caller nor self. He simply proffers the unassailable truth: "One might ask, 'Why do you always look for a cop when there's none around?'"

Dr. Science shows that he knows how to talk as Eskimos

talked before dogsleds were replaced by snowmobiles, Kayaks by motor boats, spears by rifles, and igloos by houses. In the good old days, when Eskimos operated in tight quarters, as nearly all modern teachers do, Eskimos rarely accused anyone in the igloo of having failed to do what that person should have done. Wise in the ways of lighting fires without matches, Eskimos were content to say, "*Someone* has failed to keep the pot boiling." And frequently, using still greater discretion, Eskimos were heard to say, "It would seem that the pot has not been kept boiling."

All Eskimos are not teachers. And all teachers are not Eskimos. But it has been established by scholars that "one might ask . . ." is derived from the same etymological root as, "it would seem that the pot has not been kept boiling." For old Eskimos and modern teachers, a few unassuming words to the wise are sufficient. And though it it has not been reported how the residents of igloos reacted when the head honcho said, "it would seem that the pot has not been kept boiling." I am certain those words struck terror in the hearts of the miscreants since soft, icy words sound extremely loud in small, icy-walled igloos. I do know that when a modern teacher says, "one might ask" in a well-run classroom, all sensible students know they damn well better come up quickly with the answer to the unasked question.

Actually, all teachers are not alike. There are two classes. Some know the truth and state it flat out; they are old-fashioned teachers. Others know the truth and state it without seeming to; they are modern teachers. The former talk like pontiffs, the latter, like Eskimos. Eskimos, B.T. Before television.

Dr. Science is either an old Eskimo or a modern teacher. Asked "Why can you never find a cop when you need one?", Dr. Science, knowing that his answer—posed as a question—may be the height of wisdom or the depth of folly, asks calmly, "Why do you always look for a cop when there's none around?" Thereby, Dr. Science, by dawn's early light, reminds the not-quite-awake teacher that all wisdom is the wisdom of the idiot savant. And what teacher can aspire to higher?

The Warp and the Woof

"Facts are pernicious when they do not quicken the mind that grasps them."

George Palmer, *The Ideal Teacher*

1

For stressing essentials—some call it a classical education—we owe much to the Chinese. For them the symbol for "classical" is a weaving symbol signifying the warp and, so, the strands around which all else, the woof, is woven. Chinese teachers have long taught and Sumi painters long shown a remarkable reverence for the warp. Century after century they have held warps and ancestors in equally high regard.

Some sinologists say that Chinese teachers of old, having discovered that one teacher's warp is another's woof, invented gunpowder. Others say that those Chinese teachers, like most teachers since, preferred character assassination to pyrotechnical explosion. Unfortunately, sinology is not an exact science. All sinologists agree, however, that Chinese teachers of old, whatever their favored instruments of war, were, like many teachers since, devout essentialists.

When I was starting out as a clinical teacher, the chief asked our assembled staff, "What can a teacher teach?" We knew him well enough to know he meant something like this: "Of all that a teacher may have learned of the instruments, information, and theories of his or her field, what can he or she hope to teach? How much and what can be taught straightaway? How much and what must be taught later? And how much and what can never be taught?"

Some of us were young, but none was entirely naive. Grasping quickly the difficulty of tackling the question we had been asked, and having already learned that vexing questions of possibility can be laid neatly to rest by raising questions of morality, we dodged the question of what a teacher *can* teach and tackled the question of what a teacher *should* teach. And to that deftly substituted question, we replied in multipart, if parsimonious, harmony, "A teacher should teach the essentials of his or her field." Having demonstrated in this way our devotion to essentialism, we demonstrated by the same activity the true teacher's common deficiency. We hopelessly confused hope with possibility.

I remember wondering at the time whether our mutually congratulatory accord reflected the truth of our assertion or a shared fondness for the banal. And yet, muzzled by an unfortunate timidity in the face of this vociferous unanimity, I remained silent. I was not prepared to question the necessity, still less the possibility, of teaching essentials. To do so, I feared, would risk betraying that I had trouble telling my warps from my woofs.

But it was not timidity alone that stopped me from challenging our harmonious ode to essentialism. I regarded essentialism a reasonable philosophy even if its goals were temporarily out of reach. And a staunch optimism led me to believe that my teaching would sooner or later be suffused with a compelling vision of what was essential and what was not, and my teaching would at the same time be guided by a knowledge of how to teach the essential rather than the non.

Besides, I was convinced that a confused essentialism was more to be desired than the shallow eclecticism into which it was clearly so easy to drift. Indeed, I had already grasped that if any teacher was interested in beekeeping, that teacher would find a way to introduce beekeeping into the curriculum of his or her school, whether that school was one of opera, osteology, or oceanography; and long after that teacher had left that school, though no one was likely to remember why beekeeping had been introduced in the first place or by whom, beekeeping would remain an honored part of the curriculum; and within a very few years, other schools would get wind of these improvements and soon offer other courses in beekeeping till at last, if beekeeping was wanting from the curriculum of any school, an appropriate accrediting agency would demand to know why.

In addition, having come to appreciate the particular role of a strict essentialism as a bulwark against the threat of a galloping eclecticism, I had begun to appreciate the broader role of staff sing-alongs in promoting a sense of teacherly community. And from here it was but a short step to the appreciation that, although platitudinous group expression is universal among teachers and not uncommon elsewhere, the precise content varies from institution to institution. I soon saw that where my first staff had touted essentialism and knocked eclecticism, especially shallow eclecticism, the staff of which I next became a member touted eclecticism and knocked essentialism, especially narrow essentialism. Which is how I came also to grasp that whatever the content of group recitation, nothing proves so effective for pacification of a crew of disorderly teachers as a venerated platitude; and for spreading oil on troubled waters, nothing surpasses a well-worn urging coupled with a well-worn warning. That is, I soon learned that peace and harmony among teachers are well served if there is anything at all they can all favor and anything at all they can all combat.

Some critics say that teachers gravitate so readily to shared cliché because they are faced with so many perplexing uncertainties. But necessity alone cannot explain a true teacher's extraordinary knack of pouring old wine into new bottles. In the true teacher, necessity is met at least half way by singular proclivity.

I don't want to minimize the benefits of my early participation in warp worship. But neither do I want to conceal that the experience exacted a heavy toll. Determined to teach warps and to avoid going astray among woofs, I floundered long in hapless efforts to separate warps from woofs. And even on those occasions when I thought I could clearly distinguish warps from woofs, I soon found that warps had a disconcerting way of turning into woofs, and, as often and unexpectedly, woofs showed a striking propensity to turn into warps. Besides, on those rare occasions when I thought I had managed to grasp firmly a well-defined warp, I soon found the warp so slippery as to make it impossible to pass along to students. And little is as troublesome to a true teacher than to go to all the trouble of differentiating and catching a warp and then to be unable to pass it along to a student. In addition, it was highly distressing to discover that though some students were willing or even eager to chase warps, and some even seemed bent on catching them, few were willing to accept warps that were simply tossed in their laps.

After much inauspicious, warp-centered activity, I came reluctantly to the conclusion that warps are, by their very nature and by the very nature of students, largely unpassable. Which conclusion caused me considerable worry because if warps were unpassable, I had not a clue what to do to assist students to chase or to grasp them.

This worry was not entirely in vain. True teachers are always worried about something. They are like mothers; it's their job to worry. But I think I worried too much and not well.

If I could return to that early staff meeting, I would make up at once for lost opportunity. If asked what a teacher can teach, I would say straightaway that a teacher can teach anything *except* essentials. Without any equivocation, I would declare essentials unteachable. I would bolster my assertion by quoting Miró: "The most important matters can never be taught." I would add Wilde: "Nothing worth knowing can be taught." And I would call on Emerson: "Every soul must know the whole lesson for itself, must go over the whole ground. What it does not discover, what it does not live, it will not know. What the former age has epitomized into a formula or rules for manipular convenience, it will lose all the good of verifying for itself by means of the wall of that rule."

If I had known these truths when I first tried to teach, I might have been spared much grief. But I doubt it. A pilgrim's progress is like a greyhound's compared with a teacher's.

2

> "Nothing is so trivial as treating serious subjects in a trivial manner and similarly, nothing is more entertaining than treating trivialities in such a way that you make it clear you are doing anything but trifle with them."
>
> Desidarius Erasmus (*In Praise of Folly*)

Louis Agassiz is renowned for his inspired teaching. Samuel Scudder tells a case in point.

Scudder, beginning his studies in natural history and intent on devoting himself to the study of insects, was given a fish by Agassiz and told to study it. Young Scudder went off and within ten minutes returned to tell his findings. The professor, however, had left.

Scudder turned back to his fish, studied it more, and this time drew a picture of it. Agassiz returned, looked at the picture, and asked Scudder what he had seen. Scudder told him. Agassiz frowned and left. Again Scudder turned back to his fish. Agassiz returned, told Scudder to go home, reexamine his fish, and be ready next day to describe what had impressed him most.

Next day, Scudder asked Agassiz, "Do you mean that the

fish has symmetrical sides with paired organs?" Agassiz was delighted; Scudder was triumphant. Scudder asked what he should do next. The professor replied: "Look at your fish."

Years later, Scudder reported that this was the best lesson he ever received in the study of insects. I believe it. But what has always puzzled me is, what did Scudder really learn and how did Agassiz help him to learn it?

Several years after I had left the essentialist staff, I went to work at a nearby university where the Agassiz-Scudder incident was often trotted out in that off-hand way that teachers in that institution were accustomed to alluding to great and enduring truths. Unfortunately, however, I found it difficult to fathom the great and enduring teaching truths they appeared to have fathomed. Nor did my colleagues' answers to my questions help. I was left to figure things out for myself, perhaps the way Scudder was left with his fish.

In time I surmised that by telling Scudder to go off to study his fish, by disappearing repeatedly, and by expressing dissatisfaction when he reappeared, Agassiz meant to encourage Scudder to observe his fish carefully and to refrain from reaching conclusions too quickly or casually. I surmised, too, that Agassiz proceeded so because he was trying to teach Scudder science, not stenography. From this vantage point, it seemed to me that Agassiz's intention was to invite Scudder to "go over the whole ground " and to do so as if there were no such thing as ichthyology and as if it were necessary to invent a method of piscatorial observation and taxonomical classification. Which clearly could be, as Scudder said, an excellent lesson in entomology.

Still, I kept wondering what Agassiz really taught Scudder and what Scudder really learned. I wondered in particular whether Scudder could have been so impressed that his fish had "symmetrical sides and paired organs."

I couldn't quell the suspicion that Scudder had figured out, read, or otherwise learned what Agassiz wanted to hear and told it to him to get him off his back. It seemed to me quite possible that Agassiz had tossed Scudder a fish and then rewarded Scudder for acting like a trained seal; in which case,

Scudder may have learned patience, perseverance, obedience and other virtuous practices, but not science.

Scudder was undoubtedly bright. He may really have made the exhilarating discovery that his fish had "symmetrical sides and paired organs." But having my doubts, I was forced to fall back on my experiences as a student. I remembered that the fishes we studied in Comparative Anatomy and Embryology reeked of formaldehyde and that the "best lesson" I received was to stay away from embalmed fish. I also remembered being assigned *Moby Dick* in freshman English, being asked to tell what impressed us most, and being taught that Moby Dick was not just a whale but a metaphor. Our English teacher would never have been impressed if any of us had found it impressive that Moby Dick had "symmetrical sides and paired organs."

I had other reasons for being skeptical about the "What impresses you most?" method of teaching. In Art History, we were shown slides of the *Mona Lisa*, asked what impressed us most, and helped to be most impressed that Mona had an enigmatic smile and that her eyes followed you no matter from what angle or distance you viewed her. To this day, I cannot look at her picture without recalling those questionable answers to that question I would never have asked but to which I was afraid not to give the right answer. Still, in the case of both Moby and Mona, and in similar cases of "Guess what I'm thinking" teaching, I received good practice in guessing what went on in the minds of others, which proved highly beneficial later when I became engaged in the practice of psychoanalysis.

I don't know why my colleagues were so impressed by the Agassiz-Scudder incident. But what impresses me most about the "What impresses you most?" method of teaching is that any true teacher, with the aid of this simple tool, can learn to teach students to appear as inquirers while actually working as scriveners. And few will be the wiser.

On Creativity, Discipline, and Other Desiderata

In a commencement address nearly a century ago, President Lowell of Harvard University proclaimed proudly, "When we find a spark of creativity in a student, we water it." In his exquisite faux pas, Lowell fashioned a larger-than-Harvard veritas: the devoted true teacher is a devoted spark-waterer.

Two centuries ago in *Discourses on Art*, Sir Joshua Reynolds said: "I would chiefly recommend that an implicit obedience to the Rules of Art, established by the great Masters should be exacted from the young Students. That those models, which have passed through the approbation of ages, should be considered by them as perfect and infallible guides, as subjects for their imitation, not their criticism."

"I am confident," he continues, "that this is the only efficacious method of making a progress in the Arts; and that he who sets out with doubting will find life finished before he becomes master of the rudiments. For it may be laid down as a maxim, that he who begins by presuming on his own sense, has ended his studies as soon as he has commenced them. Every opportunity, therefore, should be taken to discountenance that false and vulgar opinion, that rules are the fetters of genius. They are fetters only to men who are no genius, as that armour, which upon the strong is an ornament and a defense, upon the weak and the misshapen, becomes a load, and cripples the body it was meant to protect."

Sir Joshua concludes, "How much liberty may be taken to break through those rules, and as the poet expresses it: to snatch a grace beyond the reach of Art, may be a subsequent consideration, when the pupils become masters themselves. But let us not destroy the scaffold, until we have raised the building."

Sir Joshua Reynolds is an unending inspiration. Given a single student bent on dodging the drudgery of learning the essentials of any field, whether a drudgery inherent in the subject or in the teacher's ways of teaching, and given, in particular, one student who proposes to express his or her 'creativity' without mastering those essentials, the true teacher inflicts on all students all measures needed to cope with the one student's misconception.

This is but one piece of a larger policy of teacher largesse. On finding what one student needs under unusual circumstances, the true teacher provides it to all under all circumstances. Our credo is "All for one and one for all." We are always prepared to go the extra mile.

Of the importance of tapering off students who are feeling their oats, Reynolds also says, "The Directors ought more particularly to watch over the genius of those students, who being more advanced, are arrived at that critical period of study, on nice management of which their future turn of taste depends. At that age, it is natural for them to be more captivated with what is brilliant than what is solid, and to prefer splendid negligence to painful and humiliating exactness."

Through his discourses, Reynolds has riveted forever the true teacher's attention on trouble-making students who aspire to what they call "originality" before learning what we call "discipline." And true teachers use such rivets to build the sturdiest schools. For example, following Reynolds, teachers in the best British schools of watercolor painting taught their craft by limiting students to painting for no less than a year in sepia, or to painting cloud studies, or to painting cloud studies in sepia. On seeing the success of these British teachers of watercolorists, and on recognizing the efficacy of their scaffold-first method, thousands of teachers in other fields soon were engaged all over the world in scaffold-firsting. By these means, they watered effectively many sparks of creativity. Furthermore, many teachers of that aqueous ilk then and later bolstered their briefs for "discipline first" and "creativity later" by calling attention to the careers of Demosthenes, Leonardo, Picasso, Caruso, Homer, Turner, Mozart, Beethoven, Berlioz, Copeland, Najinski, Benny Goodman, Pavarotti, Fred Astaire, Toscanini, Yo Yo Ma, and Larry Bird.

Some teachers object that to make the case for this or any approach by pointing to the careers of genius is to stack the deck. Genius, they say, can survive the most abysmal teaching practices and come out genius. Others note that, on one hand, scaffold-firsters claim there can be no creativity without discipline and that therefore by imposing discipline they set the stage for creativity, and, on the other, they claim that creativity is beyond any teacher's power to foster and that they therefore simply teach what can be taught and let creativity take care of itself. One way, they take credit for the creativity that sometimes develops; the other, they surrender all claim to credit and avoid all blame for creativity's rarity. Nevertheless, whatever partial truth there may be in these criticisms, no judicious observer will blame Reynolds for the excesses of his followers. Rather, the judicious observer will recognize that all true teachers are beholden to Reynolds for teaching them how to lay down the law with panache.

But no two teachers will teach a discipline, or invite discipline, the same way. Many teachers follow Reynold's lead by putting discipline first and creativity second; but many put creativity first and discipline second. And as much as the discipline-firsters have learned from Reynolds, the creativity-firsters have learned from Ranier Maria Rilke.

In 1902, a young man of nineteen sent his poems to Rilke for an opinion. Rilke replied, "You ask whether your poems are good. You ask me. You have asked others before. You send them to magazines. You compare them with other poems and you are disturbed when certain editors reject your efforts. Now (since you have allowed me to advise you) I beg you to give all that up. You are looking outward and that, above all, you should not do now. Nobody can counsel and help you, nobody. There is only one single way. Go into yourself."

Rilke added, "After all, I do only want to advise you to keep growing quietly and seriously throughout your whole development; you cannot disturb it more rudely than by looking outward and expecting from outside, replies to questions that only your inmost feeling in your most hushed hour can perhaps answer."

Admirers of Rilke find his advice the unmistakably practical advice only an unmistakably romantic poet-teacher can give to a would-be poet. They say the advice of the scaffold-firsters is fit only for would-be hacks.

In any case, although to the Reynold's follower or to the casual observer, Rilke's advice might seem easier given (and taken) than Reynolds', all true teachers will marvel at Rilke's feat. They will know how extraordinary it is for a poet-teacher to be able to refrain from inflicting marks on another's poetry and from telling the other straightaway—especially when the other has asked for it—how the other's poetry could be improved. Besides, they will know how hard it is for a poet-teacher to refrain from telling the other straightaway, whether the other has asked for it or not, whether the other is cut out to be a poet.

Rilke followers say it was not for lack of a teacher's license that Rilke refrained from judging the young man's poetry. Rilke, they say, had a higher license: the license not to teach, that is, not to teach as Sir Joshua taught. But Reynolds followers say Rilke followers expect capacities for self-scrutiny and for do-it-yourself learning that few students possess.

Reynoldsians say Rilkeans fail to teach what needs teaching and if Rilkean teaching seems useful it is simply because Reynoldsians have taught yesterday, or will teach tomorrow, what Rilkeans fail to teach today.

From the long duration of this acrimonious quarrel—a quarrel that seems resolvable—it might be concluded that teachers never learn. But that conclusion would, I believe, be mistaken. Time and teachers have not stood still. Yesterday, the Reynolds-Rilke controversy was heated; today it ranges from tepid to cold. Today most teachers regard it foolish to oppose "scaffold" to "invention"; they know there's no creativity without discipline and no discipline without creativity. And today, knowing full well the folly of pitting discipline against creativity, the true teacher, with an educated blend of discipline and creativity, uses both Reynoldsian and Rilkean ways to water the sparks of creativity.

A Concise History of Teaching

"For every problem, there's a solution, short, simple, and wrong."

H.L. Mencken

THE GREEKS

For scholarly teachers, the lessons of history are obligatory. In timeless conversation with sage minds past, we seek fresh insights into the present and future. Repeatedly traversing familiar terrain, we exult in the unending discovery that we have reached new and higher plains with longer and broader perspectives.

We regard such heady conversations the hallmark of a liberal education. Nor are these conversations the elitist expressions multicultural critics make them out to be. The true teacher invites all students to indulge in the very same civilized conversations with the very same select persons.

Long before Santayana, the true teacher knew that to understand today you must understand yesterday. Moreover, the true teacher has long known there's no better way to understand yesterday than to converse with the great minds of yesterday and to converse with the great minds of today conversing with the great minds of yesterday.

Still, despite impressive devotion to the study of history, and especially to the history of generals, teachers have devoted surprisingly little attention to the history of teaching. Despite diligent search, I have failed to discover a single satisfactory account of the history of teachers and teaching. I have been forced, therefore, to undertake my own.

A thorough study would probably begin with the habits of teachers who painted on the walls of caves and so paved the way for the later classroom use of slate and chalk. The thorough historian might turn next to teachers who carved their lessons in stone: first in high relief, then in low, and then sinking still lower, in cuneiform. I've been forced, however, by the limitations of a teacher's schedule to confine my studies to a few representative teachers whose activities have been set down in bookish print. For simplicity, I began with the Greeks.

The most renowned early Greek teachers were teachers of philosophy. Which stands to reason because no teacher can long endure without becoming a philosopher.

The early Greek philosopher-teachers were dedicated to teaching what we now call the Greek virtues. But the Greek philosopher-teachers never called those virtues Greek because they made such a virtue of avoiding hubris. Moreover, in their approach to teaching, they made a special virtue of going beyond the aim of imparting information and of trying to impart the art of using that information well. They tried, that is, to impart not merely information but wisdom. And wisdom, in their books, and especially in their lectures, was knowledge and the love of knowledge informed by virtuous intent.

When I first read about those lofty agendas, they looked pretty good. But that was before I read Lucien.

From Lucien I learned how those early humanist teachers
went about teaching virtue. Lucien says those teachers taught
by lecturing hour after hour to huge crowds of captive students. And this cruel and unusual punishment was thought to
be acceptable, even honorable, in the very same city nations
that regarded themselves the cradles of democracy. What's
more, Lucien says that these polytheistic moralists often talked
nonstop for as long as six to nine hours. (Which is a record for
nonstop moral lecturing that has never since been matched
except by monotheistic Protestant teachers in late eighteenth-
and early nineteenth-century America.)

In short, I learned from Lucien that those early Greek
philosopher-teachers may have taught moral wisdom valiantly,
but they failed completely to teach it compassionately.
Grasping that failure, and seeing the gap between their
avowed moral intent and their immoral ways of teaching, I
decided it was folly to expect to learn anything about teaching
from those early Greek philosopher-teachers except how not to
go about it.

In time, I realized I had been a bit hasty. I realized that the
students of those teachers, by being forced to listen to such
protracted harangues, learned to practice several of the virtues
about which they were so continuously and unvirtuously ha-
rangued. They learned, for example, to practice patience, perseverance, and politeness. (It was probably in those circumstances that Zeno got his inspiration for Stoicism.) Moreover, it
can be no accident that in the face of the unimaginative practices
by which they were taught, so many students developed their
imaginations: artistic, literary, scientific, and other. Which may
be the real secret of that Golden Age of Greek creativity. How
better to encourage the pursuit of fantasy than to subject students to those long-winded lectures? How better to give students practice in seeming to be listening while actually gazing
to vistas beyond? And what know-how is of larger advantage,
in school or out, than to know how to seem to be attending to
one thing while actually attending to another?

Nor did the advantages of those lectures stop there. To the
extent they proved stifling both to students and teachers, they

stimulated a few far-seeing young Turks among the Greek philosopher-teachers to move toward outdoor teaching. And that outdoor teaching, for which Greek philosopher-teachers have become justly renowned, constituted an effort not only to meet students where their minds were but, by exposing them to Mediterranean aeration, to rouse them from the soporific effects of prolonged indoor lecturing. Moreover, this alfresco teaching led eventually to the widespread Greek preference for peripatetic teaching in which the beneficial effects of fresh air were supplemented by those of walking.

I was helped by these discoveries to grasp a fundamental principle of teaching: the worst teaching often leads to the best consequences and the best teaching to the worst. In teaching and learning, one thing leads to another and another; and in teaching and learning serendipity reigns supreme. Which is why teachers intuited chaos theory long before twentieth-century science got into the act.

All of which makes clear why Socrates came along with his now famous Socratic method. Without the existing system of long lecturing, there would have been no need for Socrates. With that system, if there had been no Socrates, it would have been necessary to invent one.

Insofar as Socrates was a conformist, his peripatetic teaching advanced the first steps from indoor lecturing toward outdoor walking and talking. He simply exploited the existing circumstance that the Greeks were suckers for anything that promised to develop a sound mind in a sound body.

Insofar as Socrates was a radical, which he was not much, his peripatetic method enabled him to teach outside school, where he would be observed less readily than inside. Plato suggests that Socrates, emboldened by his change of teaching venue and moved to defy the tradition of handing down the word, encouraged students to think for themselves. Plato also suggests that Socrates, grasping that truth and a love of truth cannot be handed down as a commodity, resolved not to teach by dispensing answers but instead by posing questions.

At first I was stirred by Socrates' promising interrogations. I regarded Socratic questions the long awaited answer to the question of how to help students to pursue woofs in order to grasp warps. Experience, however, proved the better teacher. I came to the realization that with a modicum of practice and imagination, the true teacher can employ questions at least as effectively as answers in the service of handing out answers. In addition, on rereading Plato's writings about Socrates' workings, I saw what I had not seen before: Socrates' questions were never intended to open the inquiries that Reynolds would later have deplored and Rilke applauded. Socrates used questions to drive his students to the conclusions to which he had wanted all along to drive them. With a radical like that, who needs a conservative?

Socrates may have aspired to the humanism for which in his day he was discredited and for which he was later credited. But if he aspired to that goal, he failed repeatedly in his teaching to reach it. An unbiased reading of Socrates' dialogues with Euthyphro, Crito, and Simmias, or Cebes, Phaedras, and Theodorus, and especially Thaetetus, can't fail to reveal Socrates' intent, skill, and delight in leading the witness.

In the light of Socrates' predilection for indoctrination, the last act in his life was a terrible mix of Peloponnesian irony and tragedy. Socrates was done in—pushed to do himself in—not because what he was teaching was in fact so revolutionary but because his way of teaching was a trifle out of the ordinary. In addition, confusion over his activity was large, because his peripatetic ways made it hard for the authorities to know just what and how he was teaching. Which made them suspect the worst.

What his detractors failed to grasp was that Socrates' method of teaching was admirably faithful to their tradition. They mistook him for a conspirator, a corrupter of youth, when in fact he was doing what they were doing: teaching students to do as they were told. How odd, then, that Socrates' preference for attaining that end by interrogative rather than declarative means appeared to his detractors to threaten the status quo. In actuality, Socrates struck no blow—high or low—for freedom.

Exaggerating the importance of his minor idiosyncrasies, Socrates' contemporaries—followers and detractors alike—gave the appearance of failing to grasp that Socrates had invented an extraordinarily useful tool for promoting indoctrination that could pass for liberation. But after long and careful consideration of these tragic events, I have reached the conclusion that it was all along clear to everyone that Socrates was never a corrupter in the sense he was accused. I cannot imagine that Socrates' conservative detractors ever really believed he was a radical. I am convinced they merely pretended to regard Socrates a radical and hounded him out of envy for his skill in doing what they hoped to do: to advance questions in ways that deterred students from advancing their own.

Be that as it may, it's clear today to all true teachers that Socrates demonstrated virtues for which his contemporaries should have honored him. Accordingly, today, however belatedly, we honor Socrates, the meistersinger of questions that are not really questions, without whom and without which we might well be in a different business.

No true teacher will fail to appreciate that a persistent reliance on questions is a hypnotic that discourages independent inquiry as successfully as the endless lecturing it pretends to replace. Sir Joshua himself, despite his enthusiasm for drill, observed a similar phenomenon: "A provision of endless apparatus, a bustle of endless inquiry and research, or even the more mechanical labour of copying, may be employed to evade and shuffle off real labor - the real labor of thinking."

Since Troy, many unthinking persons have said, "Beware of Greeks bearing gifts." The saying has become a truism. But true teachers deplore such politically and otherwise incorrect remarks. True teachers are grateful to Socrates for teaching them to trade the orthodoxy of the answer for the orthodoxy of the question, and even more grateful to Socrates for teaching them how to ask orthodox questions that preserve the orthodoxy of the required answer. Hail Socrates. Poor Socrates. Poor students.

THE SCHOLASTICS

In the Middle Ages, teaching became simpler. A select group of teachers taught select subjects to select students by means tuned carefully to the aims of the community of which these teachers and students were part. Never again have teachers had it so cushy.

Blessed by these ideal conditions, teachers found the answer to the recurrent question of whether to convey answers or to pose questions. Middle Age teachers did both; and they did them in canny combination. They asked prescribed questions and then, disdaining shady Socratic detours, imparted prescribed answers. In turn, students, to be accepted into the company of educated minds, had merely to commit to memory the prescribed questions and answers and at the appropriate time to recite them brightly.

From occident to orient this catechetical method of dispensation swept the world as nothing had done before, and as nothing has done since with the possible exception of the method of dispensation developed in the late twentieth century by McDonald's. What's more, the catechetical method, like the later McDonald's, proved highly efficient and reliably constant at the cost of but small sacrifices of taste.

Scholars of Middle Age Scholasticism cite several reasons for the success of the catechetical method:

In those halcyon days, knowledge was limited, distinct, and stable. Each teacher knew all that was known and knew all that each student would need to know today and tomorrow. Unhampered by the explosions of knowledge that earlier and later made knowledge obsolete before mastered, each teacher could teach each day what he or she had taught yesterday and would surely teach tomorrow. And each teacher knew that each student would find good use tomorrow for what the student was learning today and would do so in a world that would be tomorrow what it was today and had been yesterday.

Modern teachers can only dream of such favorable conditions. Some teachers try to teach today as if those conditions still existed, but few have the skill to pull it off. When Middle Age teachers taught, absolute obedience to authority was absolutely necessary for survival; consequently, students' preexisting habits of obedience supported the catechetical method and the catechetical method supported their preexisting habits. Moreover, students knew that the catechetical method would help them to advance their habits of obedience and would help them in turn, when their turn came, to exact obedience from others.

Stability of knowledge and docility of students were not all by which Middle Age teachers were favored. Having themselves been taught earlier exactly as they were to teach others later, and free from the hopes for freedom that had hampered their predecessors and would hamper their successors, those teachers had a compelling respect for received questions and received answers. All of which helped them to teach catechetically with notable competency.

Current differences of climate notwithstanding, the catechetical method is far from passé. Although handmade for those halcyon days, it has since proved useful in boosting the authority of bishops, feudal lords, guild masters, kings, emperors, prime ministers, presidents, and other tribal potentates. And its utility and popularity have not been confined to realms of manifest autocracy. The catechetical method has enjoyed an extraordinary renaissance in the present advance of bureaucracy. In the United States, for example, a visit to any federal, state, or municipal office in any community of over one hundred or so persons will show the pivotal role of the catechism. What's more, in advanced and advancing communities all over the world, seekers of national or local information, permission, or possession can count on being met in the appropriate places by persons who have been taught by the catechism and who will in turn teach the seeker by the catechism whatever the seeker cares to know, and much the seeker does not.

Yesterday and today, and probably tomorrow, in all manner of times and places, a person once taught by the catechetical method, is seldom at a loss. Take a case in point. Just the other day, needing an object weighing precisely a pound, I looked aimlessly about for several minutes and then had the good fortune to recall being taught some six decades earlier to ask, "What does a pint weigh?" To which the prescribed answer came quickly back: "The world around, a pint weighs a pound."

Catechisms show many forms—some rhyme, some

don't—but the best read as true backward as forward. In the Middle ages these bidirectional catechisms were called Janusian or palindromic to distinguish them from the syllogistic, which read true forward but false backward. The Janusian or palindromic catechism's special advantage is that it proves helpful right off: "What does a pint weigh?" "The world around a pint weighs a pound," and then proves useful when the question is reversed, "What weighs a pound?", and the answer comes back, though without rhyme, "A pint."

Modern science has put the whole range of catechetical methods on solid ground. Neurophysiological research has proved conclusively that whatever is learned by catechism bypasses the cortex and goes straight to the midbrain, thereby sparing teacher and student wasteful registration, reorganization, and contemplation, and ensuring quicker, stronger, and longer returns. Which explains my tenacious grasp of the mysterious ways of the pint.

DESIDERIUS ERASMUS

Ask any graduates of Erasmus Hall High School in Brooklyn, New York, to name famous graduates of that school and they'll name Barbara Stanwyck, Billy Cunningham, Sid Luckman, Beryl Synofsky, Maxwell Rosenlicht, and other distinguished persons. But ask the same graduates who Desiderius Erasmus was and nine out of ten will give you a blank stare.

I can readily understand that blank. When I attended Erasmus Hall High School, I never once heard a teacher say who Desiderius Erasmus was, or even mention him by name, although many teachers mentioned considerably lesser persons and told many reasons for their fame. Nor do I remember even wondering who Desiderius Erasmus was.

Such secrecy about the person after whom a school is named may seem odd to graduates of James Madison, Thomas Jefferson, Peter Stuyvesant, George Washington, or even Boys' High, but there was good reason for it, although I didn't learn the reason till much later. I know I didn't learn it when I made the leap from Erasmus Hall High School in Brooklyn, New York to Cornell University in Ithaca, New York; in the latter, as in the former, I heard no mention of Erasmus's name. I'll go back to Erasmus Hall High School in a moment. But as far as the gap in my college education is concerned, it may have been my own fault. Having lived much of my life near Prospect Park in the city, and having been faced with a choice between Cornell University in Ithaca, New York and Columbia University in New York, New York, I was highly partial to the country and chose accordingly Cornell University in the country. If, to the contrary, I had chosen Columbia University, in the city, I imagine I might possibly have heard something about the urbane Erasmus. But at Cornell University, as in Erasmus Hall High School, I never heard a single reference to his name.

Of course, the problem may have been more than one of location. Having chosen premedicalism, I suppose I couldn't reasonably expect to learn much about Desiderius Erasmus from teachers busy teaching such staples as integral calculus, genetics, zoology, embryology, comparative anatomy, and organic, qualitative, quantitative, and physical chemistry. And yet it seems that someone or another on one occasion or another might have mentioned something or other about Desiderius Erasmus. I know that Hippocrates was mentioned several times and I think Avicenna. But to the best of my knowledge, Desiderius Erasmus, never.

Not till I was a student at the Columbia University College of Physicians and Surgeons did I learn the reasons for Erasmus's predicament. And even then it was not from anything in the regular curriculum. Hoping to make up for deplorable deficiencies of nonmedical knowledge, George Fisher, Burns Amberson, Larry Warbasse, and I formed the Benjamin Rush Society, an organization dedicated to the high purpose of encouraging nonmedical reading and discussing. Which purpose we managed persistently to pursue despite the dean's steadfast disapproval of such diversion of energies from the medical.

Inspired by my fellow Rushians' approval and by the dean's disapproval, I read as many books as I could on Clifton

Fadiman's list of great books. Which was when I ran into
Erasmus and began at last to grasp why my teachers had
neglected to mention his name.

Anyone who has studied Erasmus's writings might conclude he was in trouble with teachers because of his praise of
folly. But I believe the trouble lay not solely or even mainly in
Erasmus's taste for irony, parody, lunacy, whimsy, ambiguity,
and gaiety. Teachers are not entirely lacking in appreciation of
these qualities even if their appreciation may be dulled by
overexposure to class clowns. Where Erasmus made his big
mistake, an egregious mistake, was in calling upon Plato and
Horace in support of his many forms of frivolity. He said in his
letter to Martin Dorp in 1515:

"The philosopher Plato, serious-minded though he is,
approves of fairly lavish drinking matches at banquets because
he believes that faults which austerity cannot correct, the gaiety
of wine-drinking can dispel. And Horace thinks that joking
advice does as much good as serious. 'What stops a man who
can laugh,' he says, 'from speaking the truth?'"

And he adds: "This was surely well understood by the
famous sages of antiquity who chose to present the most
salutary counsel for life in the form of amusing and apparently
childish fables because truth can seem harsh if unadorned, but
with something pleasurable to recommend it can penetrate
more easily the minds of mortals. No doubt this is the honey
which doctors in Lucretius smear on the rim of a cup of
wormwood which they prescribe for children."

Could Erasmus have imagined that these extraordinarily
provocative quotations would convince his friend Dorp and
Scholastics less friendly of the propriety of his light-hearted
approach? 1515 was, after all, a very sober year, and long
before Erasmus's position was to receive support from a
popular song about a spoonful of sugar making the medicine
go down. Could Erasmus simply have failed to realize that
quoting Pagans would compound his sins of levity in the eyes
of the Scholastics? Or did he realize it, and driven by a puissant
self-destructive propensity, go ahead anyway? From his por-
traits, I suspect the latter.

Still, there is reason to believe that his choice was neither all simplicity nor all complicity, but what we psychoanalysts like to call a compromise formation. Since Erasmus was not the conservative Socrates was but rather a dedicated radical, he was in need of a better cover than can be provided by peripateticism or by the pretense of inviting inquiry through interrogation. It seems highly probable that cleverly though unwisely, by acting the part of a joker, Erasmus tried to spare himself a stretch on the rack. And yet, by that very same jokering, which may indeed have spared him that stretching, he managed to ensure that no Scholastic would take him seriously. In one and the same act, therefore, as surely as Erasmus pursued both his pleasure and his safety, he brought about his unending penalty.

Erasmus was in a no win position. If he had talked seriously, he would have been ignored because glum. Choosing to talk frivolously, he was ignored because flaky. Besides, when Erasmus from time to time tried to speak seriously, he was in especially big trouble. He said:

"Perhaps it were better to pass over the theologians in silence. . . . For they may attack me with six hundred arguments, in squadrons, and drive me to make a recantation, which if I refuse, they will straight away proclaim me a heretic. By this thunderbolt, they are wont to terrify any toward whom they are ill-disposed. . . . They are protected by a wall of scholastic definitions, arguments, corollaries, implicit and explicit propositions; they have so many hideaways that they could not be caught even by a net of Vulcan . . . and they abound with newly invented terms and explain as pleases them the most arcane matters."

Hearing this, many Scholastics decided that Erasmus meant to put their catechisms in the catacombs. Nor did it matter that he meant only to suggest that the catechetical method was being misused, not that it was useless. Because Desiderius Erasmus kidded around so much, he was bound to be misunderstood. Which is why it is difficult to escape the conclusion that the very kidding around that saved his life ensured as surely that he would be forever misunderstood.

At best, Erasmus's pronouncements had a mixed effect. Many Scholastics ignored him and continued to teach the catechisms as before. Others opposed him and redoubled their catechistic reliance. Still others, including some who claimed to be his followers, throwing out baby with bathwater, eliminated all traces of the catechetical method from their teaching. Moreover, that range of unfortunate consequences—from neglect to opposition to redoubling of old practices to mistaken application of his views—has persisted among teachers right down to the present.

Saddened and angered by his reception, Desiderius Erasmus, with some help from Avicenna and more from Tom Aquinas, went on to assert that the Scholastics, in their strict adherence to the letter of Christian law, had lost the spirit of Christianity and, in gaining a rigid orthodoxy, had lost Christ. And if that wasn't enough, he opined that the human condition is not originally one of sin but rather of grace. In voicing this opinion about original grace, Erasmus threatened the basic beliefs not only of the Scholastics but of all teachers since. He challenged, that is, what all true teachers have always regarded a self-evident and fundamental truth: students are born in need of reformation. And so, though a smattering of teachers subsequently applauded Erasmus's assault on Scholasticism, many more have deplored his aid and comfort to hereticism.

Which is why, having asserted that the Scholastics honored the icons of Christianity but forgot Christ's messages, Erasmus was himself honored as an icon by teachers who forgot his messages and why Erasmus Hall High School in Brooklyn, New York, was founded in honor of Erasmus, and yet no teacher in that school ever mentioned his name. Which is also why, honored by having his name given to a high school, Erasmus was, in that very honor, punished by having his name become a school's and no longer his own.

JOHN DEWEY

It may be odd that as a youth I heard so little about Desiderius Erasmus. It's undoubtedly odder, however, that as a child, I heard so much about John Dewey. Ordinarily, John Dewey is not a household word; but in mine, it was.

When I was a small boy and my father a young man, he accepted an invitation to form and head a Progressive school. For years, many meetings were held in our home to discuss Progressive learning and teaching. I don't mention these events to claim special understanding of John Dewey. To the contrary, I mention them to mark the origins of my infirmity. My vision of John Dewey has long been blurry.

I do remember clearly, however, that my father and his friends kept saying "johndeweysays." Which they pronounced with a major accent on "dew" and a lesser on "says." Which produced the rapidly spoken complex-compound "johndewey-says." (One reason I recall so well the sound of 'johndewey-says' is that years later my psychoanalytic colleagues often said "sigmundfreudsays" or, more succinctly, "freudsays.") I recall how confusing such a tall word was for such a small boy and how confusing it was that when anyone said "johndeweysays" some persons would smile and others would frown. I figured out in time who was likely to smile and who to frown. But I never figured out why.

Maybe I might have solved that mystery if I had attended my father's school. But I did not. For that I credit my father for discerning that combining a father and son in the same school was more likely to lead to a Regressive than a Progressive education. The downside of his wisdom, however, was that my precocious theoretical orientation to John Dewey went entirely unaccompanied by first-hand experience. Which may be why, when years later I had managed to distinguish John Dewey from the admiral, the candidate for president, and the rookie Red Sox right fielder, my confusion over what johndeweysays did not abate but abided.

John Dewey says:

"Mankind, likes to think in terms of extreme opposites. It is given to formulating its beliefs in either-ors, between which it recognizes no intermediate possibilities."

John Dewey also says:

"The history of educational theory is marked by opposition

between the idea that education is development from within and that it is formation from without; that it is based upon natural endowments and that education is a process of overcoming natural inclination and substituting in its place habits acquired under external pressure."

I grasped these particular notions speedily and easily. They confirmed what I had already concluded. And though I was a trifle saddened by our duplication of effort, I found solace in being in such fine company. Later, having first been on the side of "overcoming natural inclination" and then on the side of cultivating "natural endowment," I came to appreciate more fully John Dewey's sensible warning against opposing the one to the other; and I grasped with no difficulty why he cautioned against opposing his new system, with stress on "development from within," to old systems that stressed "habits acquired under external pressure."

But when he went on to say that to oppose the new to the old would merely develop new "isms," "new systems *as dogmatic as ever was the traditional education* which is reacted against," I was stumped. On one hand, here was John Dewey preaching moderation and warning me against opposing the new to the old. On the other, here he was branding as "dogmatic" the old systems he was urging me not to oppose to the new (or vice versa). And, yet, if the old systems were, as he said, "dogmatic," how could I resist opposing the undogmatic new to the "dogmatic" old? And why should I?

I realize I cannot lay all the blame on John Dewey for my inclinations to oppose the undogmatic new to the dogmatic old. But I think he should shoulder his fair share of responsibility.

Nevertheless, I'll say this. On the whole, I found John Dewey much more reasonable than his critics had led me to expect. Some had called him a throwback to Rilke, Rousseau, and Erasmus. Some had mocked his notion that everyone has the potential for genius. Some had said his failure to appreciate the need for discipline would, and should, send any sensible teacher scurrying back to the ways of Reynolds, the Scholastics, Socrates, and the still earlier Greek philosopher-teachers.

John Dewey, however, never sent me scurrying back. And I never found him urging me to let students run wild or even to let them call the tune. I often found him urging me to teach in tune with my students. And that seemed a pretty good tune to me. That is, it seemed pretty good at first.

I had begun by now to see — but not yet fully grasped — that a great many teachers' teachings about teaching seem pretty good at first; it's only when put into practice that those teachings don't seem quite so good. In this instance, where I came seriously acropper was when I tried to carry out John Dewey's advice about curriculum planning.

Minding his advice, I planned carefully a number of first-rate projects. And I tried repeatedly to tune those projects to what I took to be the predictable sequences of my students' needs and possibilities. Unfortunately, though, when I tried to put those carefully crafted progressive plans into practice, I found myself repeatedly pushing subjects and progressions considerably more fascinating to me than to my students. Accordingly, though I was consistently eager to progress through my planned Progressive curricula, my students, more often than not, were not. And I found it highly painful to be a Progressive teacher progressing one way when my students were progressing another.

I soon realized the plain truth. I was incompetent to predict in advance (is there any other kind of predicting?) the nature of my students' readinesses and unreadinesses and therefore incompetent to plan a useful progressive curriculum. At first, I sought comfort in the notion that John Dewey's students were probably more predictable than mine. Then I added the plausible proposition that John Dewey was misguided by a naive belief in Natural law. One thing was indisputable. Whenever I tried to carry out my carefully planned Progressive curricula, I found John Dewey had been urging me to a greater Order and a purer Reason than I could find order, reason, or capacity to follow.

Nor did it help me to know that John Dewey said that success in planning a progressive curriculum lies in planning projects in which students tackle "problems rooted in their immediate experience." If I were to set my students to building a model of the Globe Theater, or an Indian tepee, or the hanging gardens of Babylon, would that help them to learn what they needed, wanted, and were most ready to learn of what I needed, wanted, and was most ready to teach of Shakespeare, Indians, and Babylonians? Unable to fathom which "problems" in which "immediate experience" would grab my students, I was unable to plan satisfactorily any but the most rudimentary Progressive curricula, and often not that.

And so, though John Dewey's critics had prepared me to find him providing too little structure for students, I found him providing and recommending too much. Accordingly, I decided that John Dewey's impressive urging for careful Progressive planning notwithstanding, I needed to plan less rather than more.

Soon after, I felt vindicated in my decision in favor of less planful planning when I read that Lincoln had selected McClellan to lead the Northern Armies because, when he asked McClellan what his plan would be, McClellan had replied, "My plan is not to have a plan." Then I realized, however, that McClellan was a warrior, not a teacher. And I remembered that many reputable historians say that McClellan was not even a good warrior. To add to my qualms about my plan to have no plans, I also remembered that Napoleon had spoken strongly to the contrary. He had declared that before going into battle every general should plan for every eventuality, which Napolean apparently did often and well enough till he met his Waterloo.

So there I was where the true teacher so often is: in a muddle in the middle. Faced with the question of how to provide students with the materials for a progressive education, and with the question of how much a progressive curriculum can actually be prepared in advance, I found McClellan pulling me one way and Napoleon another. And johndeweysays nothing useful about those pullings. Where are you johndewey when I need you?

WHITEHEAD

Cambridge, Massachusetts, has seen many fine teachers and many fine teachers of teachers. None ranks higher, however, with the possible exception of Cotton Mather, than Alfred North Whitehead, who, though a mathematician, philosopher, and teacher, was a very clear thinker. In *Aims of Education*, he says:

"Students are alive and the purpose of education is to stimulate and guide their self-development. It follows as a corollary from this premiss, that the teachers also should be alive with living thoughts."

True teachers, coveting their inspiration straight, find Whitehead as stirring as a Sousa march. If they had their way, his urgings about the "alive" and the "living" would hang in samplers over every teacher in every room in every school. Some true teachers can do without school prayers. Some can do without pledges of allegiance. But few can do without Alfred North Whitehead's rousing reminder: "Students are alive . . . and teachers should be."

A lesser teacher and a lesser teacher of teachers might have quit while ahead. Whitehead did not. He also said:

"Culture is activity of thought and receptiveness to beauty and humane feeling. Scraps of information have nothing to do with it. A merely well-informed man is the most useless bore on God's earth."

And:

"In the history of education, the most striking phenomenon is that schools of learning, which at one epoch are alive with a ferment of genius, in a succeeding generation, exhibit merely pedantry and routine. . . . Above all things we must beware of ideas that are merely received into the mind without being utilized or tested, or thrown into fresh combinations. . . . Every intellectual revolution which has ever stirred humanity into greatness has been a passionate protest against inert ideas. Then, alas, with pathetic ignorance of human psychology, it has proceeded by some educational scheme to bind humanity afresh with inert ideas of its own fashioning."

Some say that Whitehead fits Emerson's definition of genius: "Genius says what the rest of us thought but dared not say." Perhaps so. But genius is one thing. Teaching is another.

If Whitehead believed that simply naming my errors would mend my ways, he was mistaken. I need more mending than that. If he thought telling me the aims of education would suffice, he was mistaken. My aims are not bad; my means are not so hot.

I read and I reread Whitehead's rousing warnings, but I remained a dedicated dispenser of the "inert ideas" he warned of, and I knew, I should shun. For me, Whitehead's warnings about abstaining from dispensing "inert ideas" proved disconcertingly inert. And I found little value in being told:

"The best procedures will depend on several factors, none of which can be neglected, namely the genius of the teacher, the intellectual type of the pupils, their prospects in life, the opportunities offered by the immediate surroundings of the school, and allied factors of this sort."

Quite so. But what about my genius for converting lively truths into "inert ideas"? And with which particular "prospects," "intellectual type," and "opportunities" should I be especially concerned, and with which "allied factors of this sort"?

Where Whitehead let me down most especially, however, was when he advised: "Do not teach too many subjects and what you teach, teach thoroughly."

It's not that I disdain the spare and the rigorous. Not at all. But I think that an experienced teacher like Whitehead should have known that higher authority has arranged it so that teachers are forced to teach a lot and to teach it carelessly. Whitehead might as well have advised: "Teach fewer students," or "Spend more time with students," or, as his countryman Bertrand Russell said: "Work fewer hours and leave more for the unemployed." The British are so inspirational and so throughly impractical.

I tried to take as seriously as possible Whitehead's dubious advice to teach less and teach it thoroughly. But I discovered, to my dismay, that I am quite as capable of misusing minimalism as maximalism. Furthermore, I discovered that when I taught more and taught it partially, my students did consistently better than when I taught less and taught it thoroughly. Not unlike Whitehead, I prefer not to teach smatterings; but how am I to know which smattering will turn out to be trifling and which to be shattering?

Whitehead seems to have been a follower of Occam. And Occam seems to have been a fair-to-middling philosopher. But I cannot believe Occam was an Occamite when teaching. Or, if he was, I do not believe he should have been. In repeated examination of my own teaching and that of others, I have found a teacher's best amble most often a ramble. I can only conclude that school is no place for a razor, Occam or other.

Nevertheless, when it comes to inspiration, there's no topping Alfred North Whitehead, especially when he forsakes efficiency and raises a banner high for vibrancy:

" With good discipline, it is always possible to pump into the minds of a class a certain quantity of inert knowledge. You take a textbook and make them learn it. The child then knows how to solve a quadratic equation. But what is the point of teaching a child to solve a quadratic equation? There is a traditional answer to this question. It runs thus: The mind is an instrument, you first sharpen and then use it; the acquisition of the power of solving a quadratic equation is part of the process of sharpening the mind. . . . But for all its half-truth, it embodies a radical error which bids fair to stifle the genius of the modern world. . . . I have no hesitation in denouncing it as one of the most fatal, erroneous, and dangerous conceptions ever introduced into the theory of education. The mind is never passive; it is a perpetual activity, delicate, receptive, responsive to stimulus. You cannot postpone its life until you have sharpened it. Whatever interest attaches to your subject-matter must be evoked here and now; whatever powers you are strengthening in the pupil must be exercised here and now; whatever possibilities of mental life your teaching should impart, must be exhibited here and now. That is the golden rule of education, and a very hard rule to follow."

That's vintage Whitehead. If only he had stopped with his

golden rule and not added a leaden, "The problem of education is to *make* the pupil see the wood by means of the trees" (my emphasis).

It *makes* me most unhappy to hear Whitehead talking of "making" a pupil learn because "*making* a pupil see the wood" seems to me of the same ilk as "pumping inert ideas." It beats me how Whitehead can begin by deploring "pumping" and end up by celebrating "making." And I find it hard to believe that the Whitehead who "makes the pupil see the wood" is the same Whitehead who tells me:

"Different subjects and modes of study should be undertaken by pupils at fitting times when they have reached the proper stage of mental development. You will agree with me that this is a truism never doubted and known to all . . . the reason I choose this subject for discourse, is that I do not think that this obvious truth has been handled in educational practice with due attention to the psychology of the pupils."

Can the Whitehead who "makes" and "pumps" really be the same as the Whitehead who traces so elegantly the three stages of learning: "romance, precision, and generalisation"? And can he be the same as the one who adds so appealingly:

"I ask you not to exaggerate into sharpness the three stages of the cycle. I strongly suspect that many of you, when you heard me detail the three stages in each cycle, said to yourselves: How like a mathematician to make such formal divisions! I assure you it is not mathematics but literary incompetence that has led me into the error against which I'm warning you. Of course, I mean throughout, a distinction of emphasis, of pervasive quality — romance, precision, generalisation, are present throughout. But there is an alternation of dominance, and it is this alternation which constitutes the cycles."

And can the Whitehead who makes these delicate distinctions of emphasis be the same who goes on to say that learning in the stage of precision "proceeds by *forcing* on the student's acceptance a given way of analyzing the facts bit by bit"? "Forcing"? Where, then, has all the tuning gone? Is "tuning" in "the stage of romance" therefore merely a way to set students up for the "traditional pumping of inert ideas"? Is "romance" therefore merely a prelude to the real business of "making" and "forcing"? Whitehead speaks also in this context of "weaving" things into a student's mind. "Weaving" may be nearer to tuning than "making" and "forcing," but not, I believe, near enough.

Disappointed as I was to find Whitehead "pumping," "forcing," and "weaving" in the phase of precision, I was not, as he predicted, tempted to say, "How like a mathematician to make such formal divisions." Rather, I was tempted to say, "How like a mathematician in the stage of precision to have his passion for tuning give way to his passion for pumping, forcing, and weaving."

Nevertheless, on more careful and longer consideration, and after persistent self-observation, I have come to the conclusion that it is very like any teacher—mathematical or other—to have his or her passion for tuning give way to a passion for pumping, forcing, or weaving whenever that teacher teaches whatever he or she wants most passionately to teach. I have come also to the conclusion that it follows paradoxically but understandably that we teachers usually teach more poorly—teach with more pumping, forcing, or weaving—when teaching what we want most to teach and usually teach with more sensitivity when we teach what we want least to teach. And so, with considerable gratitude to Alfred North Whitehead for his not inconsiderable inspiration, I have come to a fuller appreciation that for all true teachers—and not merely the mathematical—it's a long way to heaven.

Concise Addendum to a Concise History of Teaching

Uncle Harold was my favorite uncle. Uncle Harold was a fanatic. Mainly, he was fanatic about bridge. In most any gathering of more than three, Uncle Harold would ask off-handedly, "Anyone for bridge?" Uncle Harold asked that question at home, and I gather he asked it on his many trips to far-off, romantic places like Atlantic City, Westbury, Newark, Bridgeport, Hartford, and Brockton. And when on his return he was asked how his holiday had gone, he would reply with a slight shrug and a deep sigh: "Everyone plays bridge."

At the time, I could not comprehend what my Uncle Harold meant. Now I do. Everyone plays bridge; everyone is a psychologist; everyone is a driver; everyone is a weather forecaster; everyone is a teacher. And everyone teaches teachers how to teach. Blessed by such generous instruction, a teacher finds it hard to tell a milestone from a millstone.

Lord Ashby tells us: "The touchstone of university studies

is not to teach great truths but rather to teach truth in a great way; not simply to inherit orthodoxy but to master the dialect between orthodoxy and dissent. It is a style of thought, which at its best transcends subject matter; a style which cannot be acquired except by someone who is constantly exploring at the limits of understanding."

But Ortega says, "The trend toward a university dominated by 'inquiry' has been disastrous. It has led to the elimination of the prime concern: culture."

Many teachers and teachers of teachers, and some who are neither, tell us to test our students more often and vigorously. Others warn us that tests, and too much stress on readying students for tests, are what's egregiously wrong with our teaching. Many tell us our students need more facts. Others tell us our students are overloaded with facts. Many tell us we should teach facts first, and how to gather facts, second. Others tell us it's the other way round. Many tell us to stress self-expression and that this will lead to the grand old truths. Others tell us to put the grand old truths first and "later" is the time for self-expression. Many tell us that nothing human is alien. Others tell us such sentimentality is the road to moral decline. Many sing the praises of a "value-free" approach. Others denounce that approach as empty relativism that leads to nihilism. Many favor the Great Books approach. Others say that approach promotes provincialism. Many tout multiculturalism. Others say Western civilization *is* civilization. Many say concentrate on the past: others, the present. One—I think Wittgenstein—says, "Begin at the beginning and not before."

Some say we seek inquiry and miss rigor, seek rigor and promote rigor mortis, fight reductionism and slide into relativism, fight relativism and slide into reductionism. It's true. Long before Murphy, we learned that if anything can go wrong in teaching, it will. And having learned and corrected what went wrong, we learn that what we have corrected was not, in the first place, wrong.

Some teachers say the Tower of Babel was a school tower. Others say the voices of opposition are the musical expression of the open-mindedness of academia. The one thing all teachers agree on is that we deserve more pay. Whatever music we play, the cry for more pay is our Oboe's A.

Between groups of teachers, between one teacher and another, and within each teacher, there are many lively tussles. We pit old ways against new. We pit traditional against progressive. We pit "pure" knowledge against "technical." We pit "learning the tried and true," against "learning to think." We pit "subject-oriented" teaching against "student-oriented." We pit "discipline" against "creativity." We pit "investigation" against the preservation of "culture" and "truth." Our teaching is full of splits and pits. In *The Prime of Miss Jean Brodie*, our profession is aptly depicted as comprising a war between those who see teaching as "putting in" and those who see teaching as "leading out."

Given the many tussles between and within us, given our furors to teach, given our ignorance of the persons we teach, given our inclinations to replace students' questions with our own, given the complex burdens of our Gulliver complexes, given our large tensions between essentialism and eclecticism, given our large penchants for circumlocution and self-contradiction, given our skills at watering the sparks of creativity, given our habits of converting lively truths to inert ideas, given the many other quandaries, dilemmas, and challenges that come of toiling in ivory towers, given our problematic solutions to all our teaching problems, and lacking either a reliable guide to follow or a Sanchez as leading follower, what's a true teacher to do?

Book II

A GENTLE SYMBIOSIS

The Student
and the Teacher

On New and Old Beginnings

1

True teachers are avid students of the statistically insignificant. Through small windows we struggle to see large worlds. And this habit is not simply the consequence of how our schools are built. We work the same in school and out.

When one of my grandchildren was three going on four, my daughter brought him to Cape Cod to visit his grandmother and me. There, my daughter was inspired to help him to become a painter, a Sunday painter, like me. And though I have long questioned the wisdom of commissioning artists to paint specific paintings for specific occasions, on this occasion I did not.

My daughter set table and chairs, paper, saucers, water, colors, and brushes so that my grandson and I could paint side by side in a shady nook looking off through a gap between the tall surrounding pines toward the pond beyond, and toward the low-lying hills beyond that, and, above all, toward a cobalt blue sky with a nicely arranged clump of cumulus clouds: a scene designed to appeal to any painter, old or new. My grandson, however, had other ideas. He took one look at the arrangement, shook his head in dissent, retreated, or advanced, some twenty feet away and said, "I want to paint here."

His accents were on "I" and "here," the way only a small child, and a few gifted adults, can manage convincingly. In response, my daughter tried to persuade him that painting where the materials had been placed would be advantageous in that it would put him closer to me. But even that appeal proved insufficient.

After hearing several rounds of such negotiation, I concluded that the situation was unlikely to proceed to an amicable end. I launched into a commentary something like this:

"He's a painter," I said, "and only the painter can decide what and where he should paint." Then, moved by that worthy though not entirely original declaration of the rights of painters (later I realized I had patterned my remarks on Whistler's grand stand in his suit against Ruskin) I added, "A painter looks around. A painter chooses the place where he wants to paint. A painter says, 'Here is the place where I want to paint.' And once he's made up his mind, no one can change it. That's what makes a painter. A painter paints what he wants to paint, how he wants to paint, with whom he wants to paint, and where he wants to paint."

For a moment, my grandson stared at me from afar. Then he came over to my side, looked at me carefully, and said quietly, "I'll paint with you, Pa."

2

Some might say this incident merely illustrates the familiar principle, "You can lead a horse to water, but you can't make him drink." Others might say it illustrates the corollary, "If you don't lead a horse to water, he might drink." Psychologists would probably ponder the three-generational complexities. I concluded that my grandson was trying to teach me how to teach.

Skillfully disrupting the pastoral tranquility, he showed right off that he was in no mood to learn painting, compromise, congeniality, or other faculties and virtues I was eager to teach. At the same time, he showed me unmistakably how much I am driven, even on holiday, by the furor to teach. In addition, with elegant simplicity, he drove home the necessity of my putting in the background my agenda of teaching and putting in the foreground his agenda of learning.

Stirred by these lessons, and guided by an image of myself in a similar state of childhood obstinacy, and by others more contemporary, I realized that what my grandson was trying most to learn was not how to paint but how to take a stand against the tyranny of well-meaning others. Which was a project far grander than his mother and I had contemplated. I then put myself in what I imagined to be his place and was inspired to put into words the outlook he might have had, had he had the words, and had he, outnumbered and outsized, had the freedom to voice them.

As a by-product, or perhaps a precursor (in teaching, it's exceedingly hard to tell a by-product from a pre-cursor), I found myself less driven to teach what a few minutes earlier I had felt so driven to teach. Moreover, I began to see that my grandson was trying not only to assert his independence but to find a tolerable way to accept his mother's and my invitation to join in parallel painting. That is, I began to see that his insistence on painting at a twenty-foot remove was an ingenious effort to bridge between his needs for autonomy and his needs for reciprocity.

The trick in the approach to which my grandson moved me was that it was not a trick. I said what I meant and I meant what I said: only the painter can decide where, how, what, when, and with whom he should paint. And having said it, I saw that I also meant to say that a painter can sometimes be more of a painter in deciding not to, than deciding to, paint.

And so, while I was pleased that my grandson chose at last to paint, and particularly that he chose to paint with me, I had, with my grandson's assistance, arrived at a state in which I would have been almost as pleased if he had gone on insisting on painting afar or even chosen not to paint. What he helped me to wish was not for him to come to particular conclusions but to advance his existing questions of whether, when, where, how, and with whom to paint. And I'm sure I would never have been able to attain that position if my grandson had not made it so abundantly clear that he was seeking creative ends for what at first had seemed solely contrarian aims.

Several months later I mentioned this incident to a colleague, who declared that my grandson, at his tender age, could not possibly have understood what I said. And he added the opinion—it sounded more like a conviction—that I had completely misunderstood the events that had taken place.

It's extraordinary how much the teacher's job predisposes teachers to unseemly skepticism and how much it therefore predisposes other persons to become the target of that skepticism. Having long ago learned of this peculiarity of teachers, I'm seldom fazed by low marks from teachers. Furthermore, behavior like my colleague's has taught me never to kick a person when he or she is up. Nevertheless, at the time of this conversation, I could do no more than attempt a feeble joke about forgiving my colleague because he was obviously unacquainted with my grandson. Now, several years later, however, I want to address my colleague's objections.

I concede that my grandson may not have understood all I said. I concede that he may have understood little I said. But I do not concede that my grandson understood nothing I said. Rather, I believe my colleague paid entirely too much attention to the words and not enough to the music. And I consider it evident that my grandson, whether or not he understood all the words, understood most of the music, and on a level that lacks, defies, and transcends words, grasped that I wouldn't and couldn't have gone on as I did if I had not had within me the same tensions he had within him. Besides, I feel certain that when he said what he said, and I said what I said, we were already painting together. Which is, in my opinion, the reason he replied, "I'll paint with you, Pa."

I don't think my grandson and I misunderstood each other any more than any two talking persons inevitably do. This and similar experiences have taught me that a teacher, whether of children or adults, can ill afford to exaggerate the weight of the lexical or underrate the weight of the musical. Therefore, if I could rerun the conversation with my colleague—true teachers are always big on reruns—I would say, "If one person when talking or listening to another fails to understand the other entirely rightly, how wrongly is too wrongly? And might not a little wrongly be a little rightly for learning and teaching?"

3

It's hard to find good-enough ways to talk of good-enough states of reciprocity. The language of mutuality is full of sloppy sentimentality. Similarly, it's hard to find good-enough words for the principle of teaching that my grandson taught me. At first, I thought the principle might properly be named, after my grandson, the Matty principle. But for greater clarity, profundity, and generally good-enough applicability I decided to name it *the grandparental principle* and to explicate it: "Teach as a grandparent, not as a parent."

The difference is sizable between parental and grandparental teaching. In my daughter's parental place, I doubt very much that I could have resisted teaching the portentous parental agendas I would have felt obliged to teach. That is, if my grandson had been my son, I doubt I could have resisted overriding his agendas of learning with my agendas of teaching.

Though a grandparent cannot resist teaching a grandchild something, a grandparent has the good fortune to be possessed by inclinations and obligations somewhat different from a parent's. A grandparent is generally inclined, obliged, and happy to leave parenting to a grandchild's parents, and a grandparent is generally more inclined, more obliged, and happier than a parent to play between a child's agenda of play and his or her own. And to that properly playful end, it's fortunate that the persons who do the grandparenting are usually considerably older than those who do the parenting, since persons in a second childhood usually find it easier than young adults to meet and mingle unhesitatingly with a first.

Accordingly, it follows inescapably that the time-honored view that teachers should occupy a position "in loco parentis," is flat out wrong. My grandson brought home to me that the expression should be, "in loco grandparentis." Isn't it remarkable how so small a revelation can bring so large a clarification?

Still, in claiming that a grandparent should leave the parenting to the child's parents and stick to grandparenting, I do not mean that a parent should leave all grandparenting to the grandparents and stick entirely to parenting. Far from it. Grandparenting is not a matter for monopoly, and the grandparental principle has little to do with age or biology. Besides, though grandparental teaching comes easier in those half-asleep states that come easier if the teacher has achieved "a certain age," any teacher, whether parent or other, if willing to undertake the necessary preparation and practice, can from time to time attain the right state for teaching. That is, any would-be teacher, with the proper intention, preparation, and practice, can act as, and would do well to act as, a grandparent.

In a letter to his editor Edward Garnett, expressing gratitude for what Garnett has done for him, Joseph Conrad says, "You can detect the shape of a mangled idea and the shadow of an intention in the worst of one's work and then make the best of it." Conrad also speaks glowingly of Garnett's "putting a good face on it" (i.e., of a mangled idea and the shadow of an intention).

I believe that Conrad got something right here and something wrong. An editor, like any other teacher, when following the grandparental principle, can sometimes detect "the shape of a mangled idea and the shadow of an intention." But this is by no means simply a matter of "putting a good face on it." It's a matter, rather, of the editor, or other grandparent-like teacher, trying to help the writer, student, child, or other to bring a good idea or a good intention to fruition. It's a matter of the editor, or other teacher, trying to help the other to bring a preexisting but not yet fully recognized good idea or good intention to fruition. And that, I believe, is what my grandson did for me, and I, for him, and Garnett for Conrad, and Conrad for Garnett. It was probably only Conrad's notoriously low self-esteem that led Conrad to credit Garnett so fully for what Garnett had taught him and to credit himself so insufficiently for what he had taught Garnett.

Gumbel's Gambit

On the fourteenth of July, to cover the celebration of the two hundredth anniversary of the storming of the Bastille, Bryant Gumbel and crew were in Paris and I was at home watching TV. Gumbel was interviewing a young man who was preparing to perform a high-wire walk from the Eiffel Tower to an edifice I cannot remember. Encouraged by a few perfunctory questions, the imminent walker waxed lyrical about the freedom and exultation he experienced when engaged in high-wire walks. And he asserted with conspicuous pride that this particular walk was to be a tribute to the French revolution, the world-wide struggles for the rights of man, and similar lofty undertakings.

Gumbel seemed skeptical, both about the wisdom of the high walk and about its high rationale. In his studiously low-key fashion, Gumbel asked if a part of the high-wire walker's excitement came from "breaking the rules." Keeping a fit mix of solemnity and buoyancy, but betraying more than a trace of asperity, the young man replied, "Of course. Of course. I'm a bank robber at heart."

Then, showing his consummate skill at keeping his balance, the high-wire walker turned the conversation back to the high aims and romance of his high-wire activities. Gumbel still seemed unimpressed. Then, apparently wanting to bring the endangered fellow back to earth, Gumbel asked what he planned to do "when all this is over."

Gumbel was clearly referring to the time when the walker's career would be over. But the walker responded as if he had been asked what he would do when the day's walk was over. He said:

"When it's over, I'll be thinking of my next walk."

Gumbel chose to ignore—he couldn't possibly have failed to notice—that the daring young man was not about to imagine his career being over; he could scarcely stand the thought of a lull between his current walk and the next. It became increasingly apparent that Gumbel and the walker were not in balance. The walker wanted to avoid earthbound risks. Gumbel wanted him to avoid the aerial. The walker wanted to stay high in the air. Gumbel wanted him to set his feet firmly on the ground. The walker was determined. So was Gumbel.

Gumbel asked, "What will you do when you're too old to perform your act?" There was no mistaking Gumbel's curative intent. If the walker were "too old to perform," he would surely be compelled to be reasonable. Gumbel was hell-bent on ridding the walker of his unremitting altophilia. The walker, however, was not so easily rid. "I'll go on," he replied, "till I'm in my nineties."

And then, after a short pause, and with a brave toss of his head, he added, "I'll go on till I die."

Give Gumbel credit. He was still not about to admit defeat. In a last inspired if slightly embittered try, he asked, "Is your life insurance in order?"

To which, the walker, with a broad Gallic shrug of his

shoulders, and a turn of both palms and one eyebrow upward, and the pitying look that Parisians reserve for American tourists, replied, "Paper means very little to me."

Gumbel was pursuing admirable ends. The walker was pursuing admirable ends. Gumbel was trying to advance safety. The walker was trying to find links between his occupation on one hand and his own and national and international ideals on the other. (The French are very romantic, especially, though not exclusively, on Bastille day.) Mais quel domage! On this grand and glorious occasion, Gumbel and the aerial walker could find no common ground either on the ground or in the air. The walker stuck to liberté. Gumbel stuck to securité. And there was no possibility of fraternité.

I don't know why Gumbel carried on as he did. Maybe he's a would-be physician. Maybe he has a fear of heights. Maybe he's just not a high flyer. Maybe he's a different sort of high flyer. Maybe he was trying to turn this Bohemian into a solid, pied à terre citoyen. I don't know.

I do know that Gumbel was not about to join this light-footed fellow, in fact or fancy, in his aerial walk. Maybe Gumbel had in mind his industry's responsibility to discourage the irresponsible. Maybe he was imagining the uproar if one of TV's best known anchoring persons had failed to make an effort to spread a safety net. Whatever Gumbel's reasons for declining to address matters from the walker's vantage point, he missed, in that decline, a chance to help the walker tell Gumbel, us, and the walker himself more about the joys and the risks of walking high wires on Bastille Day and others.

Having earlier had the benefit of my grandson's teaching, I was able at once to perceive where Gumbel went astray. Gumbel acted too much in locum parentis and too little in locum grandparentis. He should have left the responsibility for the safety of the high-wire walker to the gendarmes, firefighters, and other qualified persons whose job and skill is to look after such matters, especially in Paris, where there's no shortage of blue- and white-collar workers whose job and skill is to clip the wings of would-be high flyers.

Seeing the error of Gumbel's Bastille Day ways, I was

filled with Bastille Day sympathy. His position was quite familiar. True teachers each day, like Gumbel on the two hundredth anniversary of the storming of the Bastille, find themselves trying to urge high-walkers down. My grandson taught me how to teach. Gumbel taught me how not to. For those lessons, I'm most grateful to both; and I'm also grateful to the daring young man on the high wire from the Eiffel Tower to wherever it, and he, went.

Hidden Questions

1

Having learned from my grandson and Gumbel to pay attention to what students want to learn, I have found that learning
what students want to learn helps me often to bridge to what
I want to teach. And often what I want to teach turns out to be
a piece of what my students wanted right along to learn; or vice
versa.

To arrive at such felicitous meetings of my students' wants
and my own, I have found it necessary to listen more carefully
and talk less carelessly than I otherwise might. Which I have
found easy to learn and hard to remember.

A casual observer might expect it would be easy for a
psychoanalyst-teacher to talk less and listen more since a
psychoanalyst has presumably already learned. But that's
wrong. A psychoanalyst-teacher is like other teachers, only

more so. It is true that a psychoanalyst while psychoanalyzing must learn to talk less and listen more. But by the end of the day—and in many breaks during—a psychoanalyst is fit to be untied. Which is why, outside the consultation room, psychoanalysts have an opinion about everything and nothing can shut them up. Which is also why a psychoanalyst-teacher's loquacity while teaching might serve as a warning to others.

Someone once said, I think it was Proust, "Everything's been said before, but nobody listens so we must start at the beginning and say it all over again." That's especially true of teachers. Teachers don't even listen to themselves.

Recently, I caught a glimpse of an instance. That is, I caught a glimpse of the forgotten prehistory of my grandson's and Gumbel's teachings about teaching. While musing about my grandson's grand stand and the wire walker's high walk, and about the connection of each to the French Revolution, I remembered suddenly that some sixty years past, while in third grade and but a few years older than my grandson, I had written in my journal a composition called School. And I remembered in addition that I had complained in that composition that my teachers always taught what they wanted to teach and never taught what I wanted to learn.

Looking back, I imagine that what I wanted especially to learn was something I was especially afraid to ask. Still, I think I was on the right track about teachers. Unfortunately, however, I decided not to show that composition to my teachers and thereby lost my chance to go on record. This belated remembrance may be a last chance to make up for that lost chance.

It might seem that a boy who knew so much about teachers in the third grade would never forget. But I did. By the time I had become a volunteer teacher in high school, I had forgotten all I knew about teachers in the third grade. Which is not as strange as it might sound. Anyone who could remember all he or she knew about teachers in the third grade would be highly unlikely to become a volunteer teacher, let alone try later to become accredited. I know it was not till many years later that I could bear to remember what I had known in third grade.

Besides, it has only been quite recently that I have come to accept that in trying to go forward in teaching I have often been trying to go back; which means also to accept that my best moves forward are often backward. And that is particularly hard to accept because it is so hard being, and to accept being, a backward teacher.

2

Setting out to do one thing in teaching, I have often done another. Which might seem to make me a confused and confusing teacher. But I have preferred to think it makes me a Christopher Columbus. (I know it's incorrect to wish to be a Columbus, but I report the urge for the sake of truth.)

In my early thirties, having been appointed to teach persons about whom I knew next to nothing, I experienced a considerable stranger anxiety. It was then, without so much as a perfunctory bow to my third-grade teachers, that I took my first vows to attend carefully to what my students wanted most importunately to learn. (I regard that vow without bow an unmistakable expression of the power of half-remembrances.) And having vowed to attend carefully to the most importunate wants of my students, I regarded myself already a modern teacher.

Vowing, however, is one thing and doing is another, especially in teaching. Looking back, I find that having conflated what my students wanted most to learn with what they were most ready to learn, I embarked on many chases of the wild goose. And though I gradually got it straighter that what my students wanted most to learn and what they were most ready to learn were not necessarily the same, I knew no way to translate that straighter thinking into straighter teaching. Moreover, my firmer grasp of the distinction between what my students wanted most to learn and what they were most ready to learn did not hinder me from lecturing too much to the students with whom I was too little acquainted.

Even when I later began to teach students one on one, and

seemed in a better position to learn both what those students wanted most and were most ready to learn, I was dismayed to discover that I still had very little idea how to assess their wants and readinessess. Nor was I pleased to find soon after that my ignorance of those matters was not merely a consequence of oversight but significently a consequence of will.

I found myself, that is, at cross purposes. I was (consciously) ready and willing to learn what my students wanted most and were most ready to learn, and I was, at the same time, unready and unwilling. I suspect in retrospect that I may have been trying to avoid that pain to which Major Barbara's father refers: "You've learned something, my dear, and that always feels as if you've lost something." I know that to the extent I was paying a trifle more attention to what my students wanted most and were most ready to learn, the findings were suggesting—or almost suggesting—the need for changes in my ways of teaching, changes for which I was unready.

Nevertheless, though I had begun to grasp how remarkably little comprehension I had of what my students wanted most and were most ready to learn, I continued to assume I possessed a satisfactory intuitive grasp. Accordingly, clinging to the comforting illusion that I was teaching in accord with my students' wants and readinesses, I taught largely in accord with what I judged those wants and readinesses *should* be. Nor was that approach entirely worthless. It spared me the effort of learning who my students were, and where they stood, and helped me to preserve the illusion that I was trying to and allowed me to go on teaching as I had all along while all the while believing I was not.

Somewhere along the way—I'm not clear why or when— I arrived at a first-class revision of my third-grade vision. That revision did not come in a Damascusian revelation but in a near-invisible evolution. Gradually shifting from efforts to fathom what my students wanted most and were most ready to learn, I found myself trying to fathom what my students were *trying* most to learn. And although what students are trying most to learn may not be the alpha and omega of learning and teaching, it turned out to be a pretty good alpha.

One change soon led to another. Trying to fathom what
my students were trying most to learn, I found myself trying
especially to fathom what they were trying most to ask. And
when I could fathom some of the questions they were trying to
ask, those questions proved a lead edge of the wants and
readinesses in accord with which I had long most wanted,
however mix-mindedly, to teach.

3

On becoming more attentive to questions my students were
trying most to ask, I was surprised to find those questions more
promising than I had expected and more promising than my
students apparently appreciated. Indeed, the most promising
questions, and those with which my students seemed most
urgently involved, were seldom questions of which they appeared aware. Rather, the most promising and most urgent
questions were most frequently asked at edge-of-awareness:
nascent questions, latent questions, quavering questions,
hidden questions, questions almost-but-not-quite-asked, or, if
asked more directly, almost-but-not-quite-acknowledged.

Not that overt questions are without merit. Unquestion-
ably, overt questions are sometimes promising in their own
right and often provide clues to the more promising covert
questions. But I have found overt questions to be, at best, tips
of icebergs, and at worst, red herrings; and iceberg tips and red
herrings can be remarkably hard to tell apart. I have found
covert questions consistently better guides to what students
want most and are most ready, and are trying most, to learn.
What's more, I have often found my students' covert questions
similar to, or steps toward, the very questions I earlier assumed
I needed to ask and, in most instances, to answer.

Having become aware of the special worth of my students'
covert questions, and of the similarities of those questions to
questions I had earlier thought necessary to raise and to
answer, I could not help wondering whether I was simply
seeing my own questions in my students' eyes. I wish I could

say this wondering was reasonable. It might have been. But I believe it, in fact, reflected a persistent effort to preserve the notion that I was the source both of knowledge and worthy questions, and my students merely the receptacle.

I do not mean that I was conscious of that egocentricity or that, if I had been, I would have been comfortable with it. To the contrary, I feel sure I would have been appropriately shocked. Perhaps excessively shocked. I had not yet learned how hard it is to teach without sliding into views that exaggerate both one's own knowledge and one's students' lack of. And I had not yet learned to detect the traces of such thinking in my approach to teaching. Accordingly, I was unready to take seriously the questions of whether and how my own expectations and questions met, shaped, and were shaped by my students'.

Confusions, misgivings, and misunderstandings notwithstanding, with more experience in tracking hidden questions, I was increasingly impressed not only by the content of what my students almost asked but by their ways of asking. And I was impressed that their questions and their ways of asking those questions made good sense in the light of their experiences, interests, temperaments, preoccupations, and preferred ways of perceiving and thinking. Moreover, I came gradually to appreciate that even a rudimentary grasp of a student's preferred ways of advancing hidden questions helped me often to stay out of the way of, and sometimes to assist in, the advance of that student's questions.

I was reminded recently of the singularity of students' ways of advancing their hidden questions and of advancing other aspects of learning when I learned that a little girl of my acquaintance—a little girl attending one of those up-to-date schools where arithmetic is taught by the latest "hands-on" methods—had trouble doing her sums till it was realized by her teacher that the child was more comfortable with numbers as abstractions and less comfortable with the school's prescribed manual manipulations and accordingly did better when spared the school's preferred teaching method and when permitted, "as if older," to add and subtract in her head.

On Catching Burrs

Some teachers prefer to begin each day with a nicely defined plan for carrying out their teaching. I do not.

Robert Frost said the starting point for a poem is a burr that catches the walker as he passes through a field. I have found that nothing interferes so much with my being caught by the burr of students' hidden questions as planning to "cover" a given subject on a given day. To be caught by the burrs of hidden questions, I must be half-asleep. And nothing interferes so much with attaining an apt half-asleepness as a head full of lively plans.

I might never have made this discovery of the importance of a mind adrift had I not arrived at grandparental circumstances. Consequently, I cannot claim the credit due a teacher who makes the discovery earlier.

It may seem odd that I took so long to grasp the importance of teaching with a mind adrift. In psychoanalyzing, I had long known the necessity of tempering importunate urges toward planning, clear thinking, and related workperson-like actions and attitudes. And in trying to tune to patients' hidden questions, I had long known the necessity of overcoming the disruptive pulls of professional gravity. I had even written a book illustrating these matters; and, a particularly kind critic had found convincing evidence in my writing of my abiding faith in drift and disarray. Still, for many years, I failed to apply these visions and skills to teaching.

My failure was not, I believe, a mere instance of the left brain not knowing what the right brain was doing. Nor was it the product of ordinary inattention nor the contempt familiarity is reputed to breed. It was the distinct and direct consequence of an abiding concern that if I paid attention to my students as I paid attention to my patients, I might carry on with my students as if my students were my patients, and perhaps with my patients as if my patients were my students. Accordingly, needlessly fearing a foolish syncretism, I opted for a foolish separatism.

Whether other teachers would do well to seek burr-catching drifts, I cannot say. I can only recommend experimentation to determine one's own optimal level of disorganization. Nor can I say that other teachers would do well to match my current high level of disorganization. I once knew a distinguished psychoanalyst who, even while psychoanalyzing, eschewed entirely the disorganization I favor. Rather, he consistently mapped in his head all that was going on in an ongoing analysis and all that was likely to go on. Indeed, he resembled those chess masters who, while playing several games at once, keep in their heads a clear and precise picture of each move and prospect of the games in progress and a clear and precise picture of each move and outcome of many games past. What's more, I have known several other teachers who taught in the same wide-awake way. And one of them seemed to teach surprisingly well.

Nevertheless, I have found that my own teaching goes better if I do other. To be caught by the burrs of hidden questions while playing one or more well-planned games of

chess has proved out of the question. I can only catch students'
edge-of-awareness wonderings when my mind is wandering.
Accordingly, I find it obligatory to curb my long-standing
organizational propensities. In keeping with that necessity, I
have adopted a policy when not teaching of defining repeatedly and meticulously what I hope to teach; and having gotten
that agenda as clear as I can, I try my best while teaching to
forget it. I try my best, that is, to be a carefully disorderly
teacher.

A Brief Case of
Hidden-Question Chasing

Having first tried to be and later tried not to be a wide-awake teacher, I may tend to overstate the case for the less-than-wide-awake. Nevertheless, I find it a good case to overstate because if I don't, I understate. Likewise, having first neglected hidden questions and later paid them particular attention, I may tend to overstate their ubiquity, vigor, and heft. But I think not. I think I understate.

Where students tread, hidden questions are rarely far behind. Still, though I am often impressed by students' hidden questions, I am rarely impressed straightaway. Hidden questions need a chance to get properly set; I need a chance to get properly unset. Answers often crave the limelight; hidden questions, rarely. Characteristically, hidden questions hunker down at the backs of students' heads and, not infrequently, lurk in locations less prominent.

How much that apparent elusiveness is inherent in the

nature of hidden questions and how much it reflects a myopia of my own that makes my focus fall short—or a presbyopia that produces a focus beyond—and how much a mix of the two, I don't know. I do know that hidden questions seem slow to make their presence known, and, even when occasionally sallying forth forthrightly, they seldom appear, on first sally, hefty or sprightly. Moreover, when heftier and livelier questions do appear, they usually prove like the hedgehog between winter and spring: easily startled by the sight of their shadows and highly inclined toward hasty retreat.

If, however, it is in the nature of hidden questions to disappear, it is also in their nature resolutely to reappear. And given the right climate, one question leads to another and another, smaller questions combine into larger, and many small questions reveal they were right along large.

Some years ago, a psychoanalyst, Dr. A., consulted with me about a patient who had consulted with him. Listening as carelessly as I could, I managed right off a fair-to-middling revery. But I caught right off, or was caught by, no hidden questions.

Dr. A. spoke first of his patient's complaints and their history. Then, apropos of nothing in particular—which made me suspect it was apropos of something very particular—he said his patient had, in his first visit, lamented at length about a friend who had recently gotten "tough" with him. Dr. A.'s staccato accent of the word "tough," fortified by a slight forward thrust of his left shoulder and a small drop of his right, along with an almost imperceptible nestling of his chin in the hollow provided by his raised left shoulder and the adjacent terminal of his clavicle, conjured in me a fleeting image of the abortive start of a boxer's jab.

I remember that image well because it was then that I saw Professor Marcham. That is, it was then that I saw an image of Professor Marcham. And I remember that happening well because I was startled to see the professor, whom I had not run across since college, when he taught me history and boxing. (To be more precise, he taught me boxing when he was not teaching me history.)

I recognized the professor at once; he had not changed a

bit. But I could not imagine why he had chosen to pop up in my office. By the end of the day, however, I concluded that the pop-up had been prompted by the startling similarity between Dr. A.'s pugnacious gesture and the professor's long-past, twice weekly transformations from a mild-mannered, soft-spoken bard—a history-taking and history-reporting bard—into a boxer.

While I was with Dr. A., I did not dwell on these pugilistic particulars. I could not. They were too fleeting. Still, since I was in a highly satisfactory burr-catching drift, and in some way informed by Dr. A.'s telling gestures and my earlier experience with the professor, I surmised—the surmise was so strong it bordered on a conviction—that in telling me his tale of his patient's meeting with a tough-talking friend, Dr. A. had turned unexpectedly pugnacious.

I also surmised that in the original clinical situation, as in the ongoing rerun in the teaching situation, Dr. A. had not, as I had expected, placed himself in his patient's place, but rather in the tough-talker's place. After which, going the tough-talker a step better, or worse, he had carried the imagined tough-talk into muscular, if abortive, action. As a consequence, as he sat there before me in a pugilistic crouch, Dr. A. seemed not so much ready to understand his patient as to attack. And then another piece of Professor Marcham's curriculum vitae came back; the professor had been rumored to have been in his youth the middle-weight champion of the British Isles and to have attained that high status largely by virtue of his excellence as a counterpuncher.

A few moments later, after another of Dr. A.'s pugnacious gestures, I surmised from his near-imperceptible smile and from a subsequent transitory grimace that he had enjoyed his fractious flurry of toughness and then pulled back abruptly somewhere between bewilderment and pain. After that, he abruptly completed his tale of his patient's tale of the friend who had tough-talked him. And he launched then into a lengthy account of one of his own exchanges with his patient, an exchange in which he had behaved with his patient in several ways he several times referred to as "gentle."

I was impressed at this point by Dr. A.'s speedy juxtaposition of someone else's toughness and his own gentilesse. And I was even more impressed by his speedy replacement of his spirited portrayal of the "tough" with his longer and quieter verbal report of the "gentle." Indeed, each time Dr. A. said "gentle," his voice was nearly inaudible.

Dr. A. then told in passing of the demands his patient had been making on him. It occurred to me, in turn, that in Dr. A.'s place someone else might have told earlier of those demands and told them less casually. Which was when, or shortly after, I caught sight of the first clear flurry of almost-but-not-quite-asked questions. Dr. A. wondered—or almost wondered—about how to reach accord with his patient regarding the date to begin treatment, the frequency of visits, the weekly schedule, the vacation schedule, the fee, the policy regarding missed hours, the use of the couch, and several other opening considerations. Which is to say, though Dr. A. posed none of these questions directly, many of his remarks, tones, and gestures, along with his sharply accented reiterations of the phrase "he wants," "he wants," "he wants," led me to conclude that those were the questions Dr. A. might have asked if he had asked overtly what I gathered he was asking covertly.

I remained puzzled, however, by the elementary nature of those questions. Though Dr. A. was far from a beginner, his questions seemed very small questions in search of very small answers. I was tempted, therefore, either to question his very small questions or to answer them quickly to invite the advance of bigger and better.

In tracking hidden questions, I have often been tempted in this way to brush off with quick questions or quick answers students' seemingly small and trivial, almost-but-not-quite-asked questions. And I have often succumbed to that temptation. From such egregious errors, I have learned, however, that it's highly unwise to brush off hidden questions on the grounds of their seeming smallness or triviality.

Informed by such experience, I managed, in the moment in question, to refrain from posing irritable questions or giving irritable answers in response to Dr. A'.s hidden questions. I soon realized, however, that I had managed this feat not out of appreciation, but merely out of anticipation. I was waiting, that is, as patiently as I could, which was not very, for Dr. A. to move to bigger and better questions. But Dr. A. was persistent. Whether despite my impatience or because of it, he stuck to his questions and began to make them clearer.

Soon after telling more about his patient's demands, he told more about his own "gentle" efforts to arrive at mutually satisfactory arrangements. Which helped me to see more clearly that his patient was not a person with whom it was easy to arrive at mutually satisfactory arrangements. It occurred to me then that Dr. A.'s pugilistic gestures, his preoccupation with procedural arrangements, his stress on gentility, and his arduous practice of protesting too little, reflected a possibility that his patient had gotten his goat.

Dr. A. went on to tell of several instances of his patient's "sensitivity" and in that frame underscored—I might say lectured me about—the special importance of avoiding the error of talking in ways his patient might experience as "scolding" or "pushing (him) around." I was again puzzled. Dr. A. did not seem a person given to such definitive pronouncements on such uncertain matters as how to avoid being taken for a person who scolds and pushes others around, still less on how to avoid being taken for such a person by a person who tends to be unusually ready to feel scolded and pushed around. And I failed to see how Dr. A. proposed to say what needed saying, or to ask what needed asking, while avoiding all ways that might be taken by his "sensitive" patient as being "scolded" or "pushed around."

I contemplated asking a few questions about Dr. A.'s pacific resolution. I contemplated offering advice about the difficulties of carrying it out. I contemplated offering advice masked as questions or offering advice in straightforward declarations about the impossibility and inadvisability of making such heroic efforts to avoid offending. Nevertheless, unable to find good reason to oppose Dr. A.'s well-intentioned certainties with well-intentioned countercertainties or counter-uncertainties, I exerted another remarkable power of will. I offered no advice. I posed no questions. I kept still. Relatively still.

Many teachers might regard that stillness a failure to

teach. I regard it an admirable achievement. Many teachers might wonder whether Dr. A.'s fierce determination to be gentle was the common and relatively harmlesss determination of members of the "helping professions"—medical, pedagogical, and other—to "Do no harm" or whether it reflected a larger disorder. I myself fretted often over that problem. And I fretted especially whether Dr. A.'s concerns with avoiding harm might constrain him in ways that might do harm. Which fretting made it harder to curb the urge—an urge I worried might prove harmful—to advise Dr. A. ill advisedly what he should and should not do. Which also made it harder to pay attention to his unfolding hidden questions. Therefore my claim that staying out of the way was an admirable achievement.

Another reason for that claim of achievement is that my forbearance helped me soon after to learn more about Dr. A.'s and his patient's pickle. Here was a doctor determined to be helpful and not to be harmful, and here was a patient apparently determined to obstruct those laudable intentions and attempting, and having no choice but to attempt, to be trying. And, seeing that, I began more clearly to see that in the tension between these opposing intentions Dr. A. was grappling understandably with many troubling and far from trivial questions about how to be helpful and not to be harmful.

Dr.A. began then to ask questions—almost to ask questions—not only about how to be gentle, but whether and when. And soon he almost asked questions about how, whether, and when to be tough. In particular, he almost asked those questions in regard to his patient's current "demands"—in one breath Dr. A. called them "requests" and in another "demands"—that he change, for reasons unclear, the time of several coming appointments and that he carry out several other assignments promptly and unhesitatingly. Moreover, when this struggle over arrangements had (for the moment) been resolved, and when he was now faced with the task of telling his patient about the free association method, Dr. A. began almost to ask questions about whether to characterize that instrument (gently) as an opportunity or (toughly) as a rule. (He gradually resolved the matter in favor of a blend.)

A bit later, questions of whether to be gentle or tough reared up again — almost reared up — regarding the best way to respond to his patient's frequent departures from the agreed upon free associative approach. After which, Dr. A. ran out of questions.

Or so it seemed. Soon after, however, I realized he had not run out. Rather, I had lost the trail. Dr. A.'s. incipient questions of whether to be gentle or tough had taken one turn, and I, another. He was no longer concerned with whether to be gentle or tough in regard to arrangements and instructions. He was now almost asking whether to respond gently or toughly to his patient's rapidly expanding account of frequently inexplicable mistreatment at the hands of one after another oddly unsympathetic person.

And even though that mistreatment did not seem so odd or inexplicable to Dr. A., he decided to keep his opinion to himself. Which, given his continuing concerns about how to talk to his patient, seemed to me a reasonable interim decision.

Having now resisted so many impulses to answer almost-but-not-quite-asked questions, I could no longer resist. In response to several such dawning questions, I offered suggestions about how Dr. A. might try to help his patient to advance his own almost-but-not-quite-asked questions about the inexplicable mistreatment to which he found himself so often subjected. Which sage suggestions proved relatively harmless, though not, as far as I could see, especially helpful.

Soon after, Dr. A. began almost questioning whether speaking or not speaking was in itself gentle or tough, and whether to speak or not, and if to speak, whether to speak gently or toughly in response to his patient's persistent complaints that he, Dr. A., was not speaking enough, and when speaking, not saying enough, and when saying enough, not saying it clearly enough, and when saying it clearly enough, not soon enough. Which began to stir questions of whether to be gentle by speaking from what Dr. A. regarded his patient's point of view or to be tough (and how much and when) by offering his own contrary views. Gradually, nascent questions turned more and more on how to be gentle in some ways and tough in others, and how sometimes to act in ways that combined or transcended the two.

In time, Dr. A. asked many of his formerly hidden questions more directly and began indirectly to advance fresh variations. And starting repeatedly from his favorite antitheses of gentle and tough and helpful and harmful, he spun off large questions (some more hidden, some less) that would gladden the hearts of many teachers, psychoanalytical or other: questions about the relation of the observer to the observed, the nature of interpretation, the evidence of correctness or incorrectness of an interpretation, the facilitative and intrusive (helpful and harmful?) effects of particular conceptions, interpretations, and ways of interpreting. What's more, Dr. A. appeared increasingly eager and able, given the time and space, to go on to more questions, hidden and other.

More on the Besetting Challenges of Hidden-Question Catching

Does anyone remember Albert Francis Gionfriddo? It seems only yesterday that Gionfriddo was third-string left fielder for the Brooklyn Dodgers. Could anyone forget the years when the rallying cry was "Wait till next year," and especially the year when next year unexpectedly arrived?

In 1947, the Brooklyn Dodgers met the New York Yankees in the World Series. In the sixth game—the sort that baseball writers are inclined to call "crucial"—Gionfriddo got his big chance. Late in the game, with the Dodgers ahead, the Yankees rallied and put two men on base. With two outs, Joe Dimaggio came to bat. Little Gionfriddo, a defensive specialist who had played a bit in Pittsburgh and still less in Brooklyn was sent in to play left field. Dimaggio jumped on a fat pitch and sent a rising drive toward the left-field stands. Gionfriddo took one look, turned, ran, jumped, stuck out his glove, and, as the ball was about to fall in for a home run, grabbed it. The side was retired. The game was saved. The fans went wild. Gionfriddo had pulled off a Dimaggio catch on Dimaggio. Later, the reporters asked Gionfriddo how he had managed to make such a wonderful catch. He replied, "The catch was easy. It was only what I had to go through to get into position to make it."

Catching hidden questions is similar: getting into position is hard; the rest is easier. But catching hidden questions, though similar to catching baseballs, is not identical to it. Hidden questions are hypersensitive; baseballs are not. Hidden questions are therefore harder than hardballs to catch. In teaching it's always a long way from "easier" to "easy."

And if the catcher is both a teacher and a doctor and moved consequently to treat hidden questions as symptoms of ignorance or illness, and moved on either score or both to rid the questioners of their questions, the problems of hidden-question catching are, as I have noted before, compounded. Nevertheless, to curb such medical or pedagogical inclinations and to meet hidden questions with less corrective zeal, I have found subsequently that it helps considerably if I can catch corresponding hidden questions of my own.

If, having caught a corresponding hidden question, I can see my student as a kindred hidden-questioning spirit, it helps me to help my student to advance his or her hidden questions and helps me to help myself to advance mine. How other teachers might get into position, and how much their hidden-question catching might require catching hidden questions of their own, would depend, I suppose, as Whitehead said of teaching in general, "on several factors, none of which can be neglected: namely the genius of the teacher, the intellectual type of the pupils, their prospects in life, the opportunities offered by the immediate surroundings, and allied factors of that sort."

For my part, in trying to get into position to catch Dr. A.'s hidden gentle–tough questions, I found myself paying attention to several of my own. I became aware first of gentle–tough questions past; helped by Dr. A.'s account and gestures and by the timely appearance of Professor Marcham, I remembered hovering in college between gentle–tough questions stirred by my rapid transitions back and forth between novice historian and novice boxer. Which led me to questions arising out of other tensions between antithetical pugnacious and pacific inclinations and to still other gentle–tough questions of my earlier boyhood. At that point of remembrance, I was tempted to quit while ahead, tempted, that is, to quit while I could preserve the illusion that, although I had once had gentle–tough questions like Dr. A.'s., I no longer did. But the remembrances of gentle and tough things past nevertheless led me forward to corresponding hidden questions present. Among them were several lively questions about whether and how to teach Dr. A. gently or toughly. Which led to several other lively questions about whether and how to teach other students gently or toughly. And if I needed more proof that, like Dr. A., I had not permanently answered all hidden questions arising out of antithetical inclinations toward war and peace, I became aware years later that in setting down my thoughts about teaching I had unwittingly called this section of this collection a *gentle* symbiosis.

Some Added Questions
on the Question of
What Attention to Hidden
Questions Is Good For

By underscoring the importance of doing nothing to obstruct the advance of students' hidden questions, I may have given the impression I teach absolutely nothing. But that is not, I believe, absolutely true. I think it nearer the truth to say that in tracking hidden questions I have had to learn to do more of nothing in order to do more of something. And I have found that one distinct advantage of being in a grandparental drift, of perusing my pictures, and of trying to catch hidden questions—my students' and my own—is that while helping me to do less, it keeps me busy enough to enjoy it, which helps me to get into position to catch more hidden questions, my students' and my own.

The question of what to do with hidden questions once caught is much harder than the question of how to catch them. One subject must be taught one way; another subject must be taught another. Besides, the teacher who prefers to be declarative will prefer to greet hidden questions declaratively; the teacher who prefers to be inquisitive will prefer to greet them inquisitively. And one teacher will prefer to declare or to question one way; another teacher will prefer to do it another. My own preference is not to respond explicitly to my students' hidden questions but to play off those questions indirectly with a mix of my own questions and declarations. And I prefer to place that mix within the broad category of teacherly responses known technically as "that reminds me of a story."

When I have talked to colleagues about trying to teach in harmony with hidden questions—trying to teach whatever particular subject in whatever particular way—I have managed often, despite repeated disclaimers, to portray myself as an inveterate advocate of laissez-faire-ism or other doctrines of watchful-neglectism. Therefore, I want to protest—but not too much—that I am not.

Recently I attended a workshop on teaching. Some teachers were strong on "teaching facts." (Several called it teaching "nuts and bolts.") Some were strong on "teaching students." Some said more demands should be made on students. Some said students were already faced with too many demands. None of these teachers was a teacher in my field, but many reminded me of teachers in my field. Therefore I felt very much at home. Encouraged by this sense of familiarity, I spoke of my struggles to catch and to teach in accord with hidden questions, and I offered as an example the case of Dr. A.

In response to that example, one teacher declared there was no need for a student to proceed in such roundabout efforts to reinvent the wheel. Another declared that even if advancing inquiry is a legitimate ultimate goal, that goal can be achieved only after a thorough initial grounding of the student in fundamentals, after which, and in the light of which, the student might then be able to begin to advance a few well-enough informed questions. Another suggested that if advancing inquiry had been the goal, a goal she felt I had in any case grossly overstated, it would have been better to ask the student probing questions, questions having the dual advantage of leading the student to the fundamentals of the subject at hand and, at the same time, demonstrating the proper way to raise proper questions. Among these teachers, a distinguished group, there was general agreement that students, with rare exceptions, cannot be expected to advance good questions, directly or indirectly, overtly or covertly, in a field those students have not yet comprehended.

I tried to persuade my colleagues that trying to help students to advance their hidden questions—to advance even inefficient, imprecise, and ill-informed questions—can provide those students a chance to learn not merely what their predecessors in the field have questioned, and how those predecessors have answered those questions, but how to go about advancing their own questions to find common ground between their questions (and answers) and the accumulated questions (and answers) of that field. My colleagues did not find my position persuasive. Nor did they find it persuasive when I added the opinion that you cannot teach a new dog old tricks.

That is not to say my colleagues were disapproving. To the contrary. Several asked for more details and, after hearing me out, became quite enthusiastic. One complimented me for having students whose commitment and good habits of learning enabled me to teach so little. One said I had done what any good teacher does so it wasn't anything new. Another, after asking more about what I had said to help my student to advance hidden questions, pointed out, with unmistakable relief, that despite my stress on hidden questions, despite my insistence that I do not teach, and despite my underestimation of the importance of what can be taught and of what I teach, I had in several ways taught several things my student clearly needed to be taught.

There is nothing more encouraging to a true teacher than the enthusiastic appreciation of colleagues. At this time, however, I shall not lug in other testimonials from colleagues regarding the virtues of tracking hidden questions and of teaching, one way or another, in accord with those tracks. I shall instead try to rest content with recalling what Ben Franklin replied to a skeptic's challenging question regarding the utility of electricity:

"For what is a newborn babe good?"

On Passing Events

In search of hidden questions, I have found it useful to pay special attention to the peripheral, tangential, and parenthetical. I have found it particularly useful to pay special attention to what my students have said and done peripherally, tangentially, and parenthetically inside the teaching situation as they have talked of events outside.

I didn't set out to set up such a watch. My attention has been pulled in that direction as a consequence of my repeatedly finding pressing hidden questions concealed and revealed in what students did or said peripherally, tangentially, and parenthetically as they talked of patients perceived and addressed elsewhere, writings read elsewhere, reports written elsewhere, conferences attended elsewhere, feelings felt elsewhere, ideas pondered elsewhere, and wonderings wondered elsewhere.

Understandably, the events of which my students have told most often and most directly have been the events we were meeting to consider: events that took place in their consultation rooms. But while my students have been telling of the events in those analytic situations, I have frequently found my attention drawn particularly to the events taking place at that moment in our teaching situation. And those events have frequently proved more telling of my students' hidden questions concerning the events in their consultation rooms than have the events of which they have told more directly.

What's more, the most telling of inside events have often taken place as students were telling of outside events that appeared far removed from the matters we were meeting to consider. Given time to unfold, however, those apparently far removed events often provided valuable clues to the liveliest hidden questions regarding the matters we had met to consider. In addition, it has often been the case that those lively questions, as if taking a leaf from the Purloined Letter, have hidden themselves effectively by positioning themselves openly in the peripheral, tangential, and parenthetical.

A student began by telling of a tornado warning she had heard on the radio on the way to my office. It was a warning for a remote area in the western part of the state and in states west of that. I regarded her remarks merely polite prefatory remarks about the weather. And yet, though I could appreciate the importance of the warning to citizens of the areas involved, and to public spirited citizens of areas involved less directly, I could not understand why my student went on at such length and with such concern about the tornado about to hit the western part of Massachusetts and points west of that. (Citizens of Eastern Massachusetts seldom go beyond Worcester in their concerns and, frequently, not as far West as that.)

Later, however, it dawned on me why my student was so preoccupied with this warning about a tornado in a place so remote. While telling of a seemingly innocuous comment her patient had made to and about her, my student wrinkled her brow, lifted her eyebrows, dilated her pupils, (and, I believe, her nostrils), stiffened her body, and reared back in her seat. Which struck me as close kin to what she had done when telling of the tornado warning. It struck me too at that moment that she was struggling with a particularly sprightly hidden question about whether her patient was on the verge, which he seemed to me to be, of an outburst of rage toward her. Or, rather, it struck me that the question was not whether the stormy weather would come, but when. A tornado warning indeed, and far from remote.

Soon after, I learned something my student had known but failed to mention: her patient was from West Newton. A tornado from the west, indeed. What's more, my student's almost-but-not-quite-asked question about an impending storm of rage, turned out to be but one of many hidden questions about the possible comings of other risky storms of emotion and of many hidden questions about possible ways to stay out of their way.

Another student opened with a cryptical parenthetical comment about a TV program he had watched the night before. The program had devoted scrupulous attention to a prominent member of the British Parliament who was said to have committed a sexual misdeed with a prominent lady of the night. Ordinarily I find cryptical parenthetical comments particularly good clues to hidden quizzicals, but this time I did not.

That is, I did not find a good clue till well into the hour; at which point I remembered my student's opening aside about the possibly errant member of the British Parliament and I realized at last that my student had over and over been circling around worrisome questions about whether he himself had committed a misdeed with the patient of whom he was telling. I then found it apparent, though he did not say it flat out, that he was worried whether he had called his patient's attention too abruptly and insistently to a possible sexual symbol in one of her dreams. And he seemed to regard that interpretive deed, if he had done what he feared, a sexual misdeed. It later turned out that this concern met part way his patient's even more distressing though better hidden concern that he had egregiously assaulted her with this and several other comments she regarded inappropriate and intrusive sexual commentary.

Soon after, I realized that these hidden questions were not merely questions of whether he had committed a misdeed, but, if so, which and why, and whether I, like the TV documentarians, would chastise him roundly, and still worse, bring the matter to the attention of still harsher authority. And those questions foreshadowed a long series of questions about other possibly putative interpretive misdeeds and other possibly punitive consequences. Many of these hidden questions proved highly productive. Indeed, much of his learning, perhaps most, seemed over and over to begin with, be guided by, and benefit from the pursuit of his many hidden questions regarding possible misdeed and penalty.

Still another student started things off with what I considered a long digression about an article she had read in a professional journal. She said in an aside that she had found the author of that article "incisive." Her expression and tone made it clear she had found the author *admirably* "incisive." I remember her comment especially because the person she referred to was one I had usually found *deplorably* incisive.

My student paused and then moved abruptly to the events about which she apparently wished to consult. I wondered (silently) whether she might be hoping I would be as incisive as the author of that praiseworthy article. I wondered also (and also silently) whether she might be hoping she could be as incisive. I found some evidence to support the former conjecture and more to support the latter. Soon after, I surmised that she was wrestling with several almost-but-not-quite-asked questions about how she might have been more incisive with her patient on a particular occasion and how she might in the future be more incisive in readdressing the matter about which she thought she had, on the occasion in question, commented—she called it "meandered"—inconclusively. In subsequent sessions, these hidden questions about this particular matter on this particular occasion were followed by hidden questions about how she might become more incisive about other matters and, particularly, more incisive when she regarded her views unwelcome. This sequence of questions was followed within a few weeks by questions about how and when it might be better to be incisive with her patient and how and when it might be better not to. Which soon led to related questions regarding other patients and a little later to broader questions about the virtues and costs of both ambiguity and clarity.

Though it's not unusual for the peripheral, tangential, and parenthetical to turn out central, I don't mean that I hang out all day with my attention riveted on the p, t, and p. I have found that attending too assiduously to anything in particular makes me unable to attend effectively. Tracking goes better if I pay particular attention to nothing in particular. Accordingly, I try while teaching to forget not only my favorite agendas of teaching but my favorite ways of hidden-question tracking. To those persons who wish to become equally forgetful, I can say confidently that this is another teaching accomplishment readily attainable through practice. And, though I myself have taken so long to attain a bettering of my forgetting, I am sure that anyone who begins early enough and practices hard enough can learn to forget well enough and to do it while young enough to enjoy that success without suffering the misgivings about forgetting that come when older.

Actually, things are not quite so simple. The challenge is not merely to forget. The challenge is almost-but-not-quite to forget. Which allows the almost-but-not-quite forgettable to assert itself quickly, spontaneously, and unforgettably. I was reminded of this urgent necessity of almost-but-not-quite for-getting by a friend's recent experience. He had agreed to greet at the Boston Back Bay station a young man whom he had not met before. To make himself easier to identify, the young man had promised to wear a sweater with a large letter Y on the front. Which seemed a reasonable plan since, with the excep-tion of one day every other year, few persons appear at the Back Bay station in Boston wearing a letter Y on a sweater or elsewhere. On the appointed day, however, when my friend looked about in the crowded station he found no person with the prearranged mark. Finally, when the crowd had thinned out, a young man of about the right age approached him, asked if he was so and so, and learned that he was. In turn, my friend then asked the young man why he had not worn his sweater with the identifying Y as promised. To which the young man replied that he had indeed worn the sweater but upon seeing how crowded the station was, he had removed it and held it high so my friend could see it more readily. Which is why my friend, who had his mind set on finding the sweater lower, had failed to find it higher and why he therefore had so much trouble finding the young man with the sweater with the Y.

To outsiders these events may seem odd. But they are true. Students are always waving the expected at us in unexpected ways, and since we teachers are so apt to have in mind exactly what we expect to find and where, it happens often that we find the expected almost as hard to find as the unexpected. Which is also why we often find it hard to find our students.

Still, when I can almost-but-not-quite forget what I am looking for and can attend—but not too assiduously—to the peripheral, the tangential, and the parenthetical, it helps me to attend more successfully to my students' almost-but-not-quite-asked questions and to find both what I am and what I am not looking for. And when I can almost-but-not-quite forget what I am looking for and attend to the peripheral, tangential, and parenthetical, it helps me to attend better to what my students say and do inside the teaching situation as they tell of events outside. Which helps me to see better where the outside and the inside, the remote and the immediate, and the elsewhere and the here-and-now meet. Which turns out usually to be where my students hidden questions and my own cavort most vigorously.

Other Clues to Hidden Questions

SHRILL ASSERTIONS

In the beginning, I found shrill assertions vexing; now I find them pleasing. In the beginning, I found shrill assertions obstacles; now I find them opportunities. Fortunately students' shrill assertions are far from an endangered species. To the contrary, they are as common as those of crows, blue jays, and cardinals, and nearly as common as and usually more helpful than those of teachers.

It was, for example, Dr. A.'s shrill assertion about the pivotal significance of speaking gently to his patient that first alerted me to his hidden questions about whether to be gentle or tough. And what alerted me especially was that his assertion was not only shrill but gratuitous, and, in addition, was spiced with a pinch of paradox. That is, I was struck particularly that Dr. A. spoke so shrilly of the importance of speaking gently.

And such mixes are not atypical; shrill assertions are rarely pure bred.

I have come to regard shrill assertions as urgent efforts to answer hastily and therefore to eradicate or conceal a hidden question or questions at risk of discovery. By the same token, I regard it self-evident that if you scratch a shrill assertion, you will almost invariably find one or more almost-but-not-quite-hidden questions.

If it is true that shrill assertions reflect efforts to keep hidden questions hidden, it is true too, I believe, that the hidden question or questions in question, if not for the camouflage of the shrill assertion, might never have caught an observer's attention. In this regard, classroom spectacles are like the spectacles of politics, fashion, and statuary: coverups accentuate what is covered up.

Hardly ever, however, is it a simple step from a shrill assertion to a hidden question. Shrill assertions need careful approaching. The teacher who hopes to assist in the advance of hidden questions will generally find it necessary to pay attention to a shrill asserter's aversion to facing the hidden question or questions that prompted the shrill assertion.

Unfortunately, however, the true teacher will often find shrill assertions provoking him or her to meet shrill assertions with retorts equally, or still more, shrill. And when he or she does meet a shrill assertion with an equally or still more shrill assertion, all efforts to help the shrill asserter to advance his or her hidden question, and to teach in accord with hidden questions, often come acropper. In fact, such well-intended but misguided efforts usually provoke the wary student to redouble efforts to keep a hidden question or hidden questions hidden.

I have found also—largely though not exclusively from self scrutiny—that when a true teacher greets a student's shrill assertion with a shrill challenge, it often turns out that the teacher is trying to keep hidden a hidden question or hidden questions of his or her own. And not infrequently it turns out that the teacher is trying to deflect attention from one of his or her own hidden questions by directing attention—the student's and his or her own—to a student's hidden question and to that student's efforts to hide that question. In which case, a student often grasps what is happening and finds it easy to disavow his or her hidden question by asserting shrilly that the lost and found question is not his or her own but merely the teacher's. Which irritating assertion often contains just enough truth to stir any true teacher to still shriller assertions, which understandably frequently stirs any red-blooded student to a fuller conviction that the question in question is not his or her own, but merely the teacher's.

After long consideration of such vagaries, I have come to the conclusion that students' shrill assertions are often a ploy. Students know their teachers. More often than not, students' shrill assertions are cleverly crafted in the first place to invite an unsuspecting teacher's counterassertion in the second place, and so to pave the way for the ingenious turnabout of apparent ownership of the hidden question or questions that hide behind students' seemingly ingenuous initial assertions.

It is true that a student's occasional shrill assertion may start out simply to silence the shrill asserter's own hidden question or questions. But if that shrill assertion proves insufficient to hide the emerging hidden question or questions, the shrill asserter generally switches quickly and cleverly to the backup option of making the shrill assertion even more shrill to egg on the unwary teacher to a shrill rejoinder, which makes it a cinch for the student shrill asserter to pin her or his hidden question or questions on the teacher.

Those who are not teachers might regard such artful measures as requiring capacities unlikely for any but the most gifted students. But teachers will know that the average student, like the average teacher, is wonderfully skilled at finding his or her hidden questions in the eye of another. And both the most highly and least highly gifted students often display these turnabout skills most clearly when pushed importunately to acknowledge the hidden question or questions behind their shrill assertions, especially their shrill and gratuitous assertions, whether spiced with paradox or spice free.

And yet, in spite of these significant hazards, shrill assertions approached cautiously and given the elbow room they require often provide the clues a hidden-question-searching teacher requires to tune to a hidden-questioning student. And that tuning often proves a first step toward finding a way to assist in the advancing of the student's hidden questions and the teacher's. Which has led me to the view that shrill assertions occupy a significant position in the large class of academic events that looked at one way are impediments to learning and teaching and looked at another are adjuncts.

POLAR THINKING

In the beginning, I found polar thinking nearly as troubling as shrill and gratuitous asserting. In the beginning, I thought mainly blackly and whitely when confronted by a student thinking blackly and whitely.

I do not claim to have freed myself entirely of an antipolaristic propensity. But in principle, if not always in practice, I have come to appreciate that polar thinking, like shrill and gratuitous asserting, is a marker that often makes apparent the very hidden questions it struggles so diligently to keep hidden. Accordingly, having come to appreciate that hidden questions often take refuge behind black and white poles, I have come also to appreciate that if I can spot a black and white pole, I am well on my way to spotting a question hiding behind that pole.

The gentle–tough Dr. A. is a case in point. His thinking was generally relatively free of polar thinking. But when moved by his most passionate concerns—and when pressed importunately by his related questions (for example, whether to be gentle or tough)—he heaped stark polarities on stark polarities. And in those circumstances he would nag at those stark polarities, or they would nag at him, till he could at last find unities or transcendities. At which points of temporarily lesser polarization, his hidden questions would seem to take on a larger sophistication—at the cost of a lesser exhilaration—till he could manage once again to set up livelier hidden questions in fresh polarities.

One of the hazards of being a psychoanalyst and a teacher is a heightened tendency to blur the distinction between origins and outcomes, or as Alport called them, roots and fruits. Nevertheless, or perhaps therefore, I have come to regard polar thinking as an effort to think as thinkers thought in earliest years in order to make life simpler when something or other was not simple enough. And I have therefore tried not to leap too easily to the easily leaped-to conclusion that a child's thinking, polar or other, is necessarily more childish than an adult's or that an adult's thinking, when resembling a child's, is necessarily childish.

Which is not to say that I regard polar thinking exclusively a matter for rejoicing, but simply that I no longer regard polar thinking necessarily a matter for deploring. Nor do I deny that avid polar thinkers, however much bent on useful simplifying, often confront themselves with more questions than they can manage, more poor questions than good, and more poor questions and poor answers than might come of shadier views.

Nevertheless, I have found repeatedly that in moments when hidden questions are hidden in, behind, or around the most stark polarities, and particularly when those stark polarities are blended with shrill assertions, hidden questions are notably spirited. And, in the main, in these moments of heightened polarity, I have found that what I say or do, or do not say or do, counts more than what at other moments I say or do or do not say or do. Accordingly, I have come to regard moments of polar thinking—especially of abruptly initiated polar thinking, and most especially of abruptly initiated polar thinking combined with shrill and gratuitous assertion—decisive moments, moments of grand opportunity for learning and teaching. That is, I have come to regard such moments as revolutionary and, consequently, the best of times and the worst of times.

On Purple Trees,
Purple Cows,
Telling Right from Wrong,
and Bearing the Distresses of
Being Wrong

1

Once I had the privilege of observing a serious water colorist investigate the intricacies of color selection. Though not world renowned, she was highly regarded by those who knew her. I therefore considered this a rare opportunity since ordinarily the public sees but a small selection of a painter's works—mainly the best and only when finished—and fails to see the zigzagging of the painter's hidden questions and the elaborate play of those hidden questions with the large mistakes, and the tolerance for large mistakes, needed to get things right. Or almost right.

At the outset, the painter set down a box of apparently randomly arranged colors. I soon gathered, however, that the colors did not seem randomly arranged to her. She peered circumspectly at each pan, smiled at many, frowned at a few, and shifted two. Then, after a long, contemplative pause and after more smiles and more frowns, she carefully put back in their former places the two pans she had shifted.

I had no inkling of the principles involved. And though I had frequently heard it enjoined that it's as important for a painter to get properly set before painting as for a musician before making music, a surgeon before cutting, or a plumber before plumbing, I had never before seen anyone take that enjoinment so seriously. Moreover, though I had long since learned that my own impatience to begin painting often left me subsequently casting about cantankerously for a misplaced color, I knew that in this painter's place, my long and chastening experience notwithstanding, I would have given the preliminary arranging much shorter shrift. She, however, despite several false starts, persisted till she found a satisfactory arrangement. And I, though watching carefully, still had no inkling of the principles involved. But I was certain that the arrangement at which she had arrived was not the arrangement I would have suggested if my opinion had been solicited. Which it was not.

After these careful researches in array, the painter—a young woman of nearly five—went on to explore the results of applying several pure colors directly to paper from pan. It was clear she regarded that choice of colors and their placement on paper a matter of considerable consequence and was determined to prevent one color from flowing into another. Again, I realized I lacked her patience. In her place, I would have been eager to push on with other aspects of painting, particularly with promoting the flow of one color into another. In my place, I felt the urge to show her how.

Without consultation with me, however, she continued. Shortly after, she began paying particular attention to two sets of colors. First she explored the reds and the consequences of laying on different reds in different intensities. Then she did the same with the yellows. After that she moved on to problems of location and juxtaposition. She applied the reds to one place and then another, and then the yellows to one place and then another. And though she still said not a word, I gathered she first wondered whether the reds looked better nearer the yellows or farther apart, and then whether the yellows looked better nearer the reds or farther apart.

At this point she pursued other hidden questions about optimal location, and I got a bit lost. But I began to pick up the trail again when she explored the consequences of allowing one color to flow into another and then the consequences of mixing the two more deliberately.

Meanwhile, though I was of the opinion that these experiments in mixing were a bit late in coming, I kept my opinion to myself; and toward each of her studies I tried, on one hand, to convey a fellow painter's interest and, on the other, to offer no opinion where none was invited. Which was difficult because none was invited.

She next moved energetically to several other studies and then settled down at last to trying to capture the color of a tree in the field before us. At which point she showed a sharp change in demeanor. Earlier, despite all difficulties, she had radiated a sturdy confidence. Now pursuing her trial-and-error mixing, she grew more and more uncertain and seemed especially discomfited whenever she made whatever she regarded an error.

This seemed to me the moment to tell her that yellows and blues make greens or at least to tell her that some yellows and blues make some greens. (I wanted to introduce first principles first and not to introduce fine points till later.) But something stopped me from imparting these essentials. It may have been the look in her eyes. It may have been the way she wielded her brush. Probably it was both. But however she did it, she managed to convey that although she was not happy about her mixing results, she was determined to go forward on her own.

In retrospect, I suspect it was neither solely her failure to solicit my opinion nor solely her determination to go it alone that stopped me from imparting tried and true wisdom about yellows and blues. In teaching, I have often imparted all sorts of tried and true wisdom without invitation and done so in the face of far greater opposition. I believe what deterred me on this occasion was a suspicion that the young painter was trying to learn not merely how to get colors right but how to get colors comfortably wrong. To this day, I find it remarkable that so young a child had so quickly, and all on her own, hit upon the essence of the learning of water-color painting.

I believe that this dawning appreciation of the importance of her experimentation deterred me not only from trying to teach her to mix yellows and blues to make greens but from trying to teach her to mix yellows and blacks to get greens, which mix I was especially eager to teach since it was of that variety of information I find so appealing to teach, information I have only lately acquired. Still, despite my furor to impart some or all of this essential mixing information, I confined myself to remarking how upsetting I find it when on trying to paint one color I discover I have painted another.

The young painter looked skeptical at first. Then she appeared to decide to take my word for it. I believe her decision was facilitated by the ring of authority with which I spoke. And I believe that ring came both of my general qualifications to comment on how it feels to get colors wrong and of the fortunate happenstance of my having but a few days earlier made conspicuously unsuccessful efforts to produce a scarlet appropriate to the maple in my back yard.

I did not feel it essential at that moment to inform her of the particulars of my misdoings, scarlet or other. But I believe I managed to convey satisfactorily both that I find my failures in water-color mixing highly distressing and that in favorable circumstances I find them a stimulating mix of deterring and challenging.

My remark about my reactions to getting colors wrong might seem a sufficient application of the tried and true wisdom that misery loves company. But I was determined to try more. Turning back to the problem of mixing with which the young painter was still conspicuously wrestling, I asked, "What color are you trying to paint?"

To which she replied without hesitation, "Purple."

She immediately grasped from my air of surprise that I had not yet grasped properly the purple problem at hand. She paused briefly, and then without benefit of comment or question from me, she added, "I'm painting purple because the tree is purple."

Hearing her reply, I was happy I had not tried to teach her how to mix greens, whether from blues and yellows, yellows and blacks, or other hues. I was even happier when on looking over her shoulder at the tree she was attempting to paint I saw, in the fading sunlight, that the tree seemed to me, as it had to her, purple. Or at least violet.

Those who have tried to paint trees know that trees are not always green, are in fact rarely green, and are not infrequently purple or violet. Those with painting experience, and many without, know that even cows, oblivious to the well-known but unknowing ditty about their coloration, are often purple or violet. How, then, can we account for my having forgotten those facts and for my being so inclined toward an ill-advised lecturing on the mixing of yellows and blues, or yellows and blacks, to make greens? I can only assume that my hasty assumption that the young artist had seen and was trying to paint the tree green rather than purple is added proof, if any is necessary, of how the furor to teach can blind a teacher to truths and colors that teacher knows well when not blinded by the furor to teach; which furor is frequently a furor to teach rote truths and rote colors, which often turn out to be, as in the circumstances at hand, rote mistruths and rote miscolors.

On this occasion, having had the good fortune not to have gone off on an ill-advised discussion of how to mix green, and having limited myself instead to the comment on the mixed feelings I experience when mixing colors, I could no longer forgo the chance to teach something a trifle more technical about the mixing of colors. I offered, therefore, a few cogent comments on the peculiarities of purple and on the difficulties of catching those peculiarities in paint. At this point, the painter smiled. I had no hard and fast evidence that the smile was a specific consequence of anything I did or did not say. But taking her smile to indicate the possibility that her interest in mixing colors might now be greater than her frustration in failing to capture colors precisely, and unable any longer to restrain my urge to teach the mixing of at least one color, I suggested a way to mix purple.

I am pleased to report that the young painter immediately pursued that possibility with unmistakable enthusiasm. And though her efforts met with no conspicuous success, neither did they kindle any unbearable aggravation. Therefore, encouraged by this teaching triumph, I hazarded an even larger leap. I made a little color wheel to assist the little girl in her future inquiries into the mysteries and miseries of mixing colors.

Whether she ever found the exact purple or any other color for which she was searching, I do not know. But I am content that she seemed content with her preliminary researches and, informed by my suggestions, content with the prospect of continuing her color researches on her own. Or almost on her own. Her mother told me that the little girl had later asked, "What will I do if I forget what he showed me?" To which her mother had replied reassuringly and accurately, "If you forget, we can call him on the phone." What more can a teacher hope for than such a propitious beginning and such an auspicious possibility of continuation?

A POSTSCRIPT TO THE CASE OF THE INQUIRING COLORIST

This was one of those cup-runneth-over days a teacher experiences rarely, tells commonly, and prizes always.

While the almost-five-colorist and I were still communing about coloring, her eight-year-old brother joined us. He made it clear at once that he was less interested in coloring than in baseballing. But he also made it clear, and nearly as quickly, that he was not entirely opposed to drawing. Following a short survey of the materials at hand, he grasped casually but firmly a large black felt tip pen whose heft he proceeded briefly to assay. Then, with the bravado of a veteran batter stepping up to the plate, he proceeded to draw. Within a few moments, however, he stopped.

Looking over his shoulder, I saw that he had covered a large sheet of paper with cubes of many sizes drawn from many angles. I was impressed by his linear accuracy, his mastery of perspective, and his use of dark, unbroken lines in the foreground and lighter, dotted lines in the background, all conveying commendably an impression of depth and solidity. There was no question about it; these were first-rate, no-fooling-around cubes. And he seemed understandably content to rest on his laurels.

I, however, thought there was more to learn. A true teacher always does. And being of the view that it's one thing to practice color and design first and later to concentrate on line, and quite another to go right ahead to line without first learning color and design, I weighed the possibility—I may have put my thumb on the scales—of inviting his attention to the neglected fundamentals of color and design.

As in the case of his sister, however, I was stopped in my tracks. I believe that what stopped me this time was not merely the knowledge that some teachers would disagree with my conviction about the proper progression and would regard it better to begin with line and only later to go on to color and design. Nor was it, I believe, simply the knowledge that cubism was once a quite respectable school of art. Nor was it solely the sure manner in which the young man had proceeded. It was, rather, the absence of any flicker of a perception on my part of any hidden questions on his part that inspired me to stay out of his linear way.

I stayed, that is, till I could barely stay. At which point my eagerness to teach was heightened unbearably by the sight of a brief though unmistakable wavering of the lad's eyes. (In the trade, we call it a rapid horizontal nystagmus.) Taking that ocular wavering as an unmistakable sign of a welcome uncertainty, and parlaying that indication into a suspicion that he was seriously considering trying something more ambitious than he had already tried, and surmising that he was asking hidden questions, or almost asking hidden questions, about how he might put old cubes to new uses, I offered a suggestion masked as an observation.

I said I had sometimes seen draftsmen who were good at drawing cubes put those cubes together into figures. And sizing him up as an enthusiastic competitor, I added that I was unable to show him how to turn cubes into figures because I was not good at drawing cubes and had been forced instead to stick to making sticks into stick figures.

Following this challenging explanation, after but a few moments of concentration, he drew a remarkably lifelike, multicubed figure than which I doubt Picasso, Braque, or any of their cronies could have done significantly better. And I was still more encouraged about the worth of my teaching and its timing when several days later my New Yorker magazine came in the mail and there on the cover was a cube figure almost exactly like the one the linear sketcher had with my encouragement drawn. I don't say the New Yorker figure was done by the lad. I do say it could have been. And that experience, along with the one with his sister got me to thinking even more about the riddles of teaching.

A CONTRAST AND COMPARISON
OF THE APPROACHES OF THE COLORIST AND
THE LINEAR ARTIST TURNED CUBIST, ALONG
WITH A PRELIMINARY CONSIDERATION OF ITS
RELEVANCE FOR ASSISTING THE ADVANCE
OF HIDDEN QUESTIONS

A true teacher likes mulling and culling almost as much as teaching. When I first mulled and culled these events, I thought they merely proved the worth of the lessons I had learned earlier from my grandson and Gumbel: when trying to teach, try not to; that is, try not to teach till, after trying not to, you can fathom a piece of the drift of the hidden questions of the person you hope to teach whatever you hope to teach.

From that vantage point, I surmised that having gained a preliminary impression of the differences in the drifts of the hidden questions of the sister and the brother (in the one instance, hidden questions about color and in the other, about line) I had, after some preliminary fumbling, been drawn felicitously into trying to teach in accord with those contrasting directions in which the hidden questions were moving. And it seemed that matters had gone well enough so that if these lessons could have continued, the colorist would have moved in time to questions of line, and the linear artist, to questions of color. With a little help. Which mix of observation and speculation reenforced my growing conviction of the importance of surmounting fixed notions about what should come first in learning and teaching and what should come second.

But following this preliminary consideration of the contrast between the hidden questions of sister and brother, and particularly of the differences in teaching that their differences of inquiry had imposed upon me, I saw a similarity between sister and brother and a consequent similarity in the approach their similarity had imposed. I saw that both were not only trying to advance the particular questions they were trying to advance, whether questions about color or line, but trying to do so in the same spirit; each was trying conspicuously to get things exactly right; in the one case, in color, in the other, in line. On considering the matter further, I came to the conclusion that, while trying to advance her or his individual agenda of perfection, each was also trying to advance hidden questions about how to bear the distresses of getting things wrong. Consequently, it seemed to me fortunate that I had not tried any more earnestly than I had to help them to advance their diverging questions about color and line till I had tried, however unwittingly, to help them to advance their questions in common about how to advance their capacities to get things comfortably wrong.

All of which led me to set down in my journal two handy injunctions:

1) Do not try to teach any student how to get anything right till taking into account what that student is trying to get right.

2) Do not try to teach that student how to get right what

that student wants to get right or what I want that student to get right, or any combination of the two rights, till taking into account that student's tolerance for getting things wrong.

Soon after, I arrived at a combinatory corollary:

Before getting things right can be addressed rightly, a student must have established rightly—and may require help in establishing rightly—a well-established right to be wrong.

A FEW ADDITIONAL THOUGHTS ON THE RIGHT TO BE WRONG

Some experts would say the right to be wrong must be established in the home. Others would disagree; they would say that forgiveness is the domain of the church. Many psychotherapists would say that a student who lacks the right to be wrong is in need of a psychotherapist. Many teachers, whatever their persuasion, would say that the development of the right attitude toward right and wrong doing is much more complex than I have suggested. And some would say that many students come to school today without having learned right from wrong in the first place and so are unready, in the second, to establish the right to be wrong.

I know next to nothing about teaching students who lack the ability to tell right from wrong. My students and I have problems of a different order. My students are adept at telling right from wrong. In advancing that talent, they have received much help at home and in school. But in regard to the advance of their abilities to be comfortably wrong, they have been forced mainly to be autodidact.

My prior experience with these particular trials and tribulations of my students may have shaped my encounter with the aforementioned sister and brother, but I was at the time unaware of the many academic ramifications of the struggle to learn to be comfortably wrong. If asked at the time what I thought I was doing with the sister and the brother, I think I would have said I was trying to help them to advance their hidden questions about color and line. But, looking back, I believe I was simultaneously trying to help them to advance their hidden questions about how to be comfortably wrong and accordingly to advance their efforts to secure their rights to be wrong. Moreover, I now believe that the seeming precondition of the establishment of the right to be wrong and of the related capacity to be comfortably wrong—the seeming precondition for advancing learning and teaching of line and color or whatever—may actually be an end for which the assisting of hidden questions, and the consequent tempering of the promiscuous urge to impart information, may be precondition.

Oppenheimer often said, "The business of science is to prove itself wrong." I think that's wonderful. But I have known few persons in either the arts or the sciences who have had any interest whatsoever in gathering that proof, and still fewer who have been particularly adept at it, or, for that matter, particularly eager for such adeptness. In both the arts and the sciences, the large majority of teachers and students I have known have seemed much better at, and seemed much to prefer being better at, proving others wrong. Accordingly, Oppenheimer might have said even more rightly, "It's the business of science to prove others wrong."

I have found it risky to assume that a student comes with a firmly established capacity, or with a firmly established wish, to prove himself or herself wrong. I am not talking about hangdogism. A fair number of students have learned, and been helped, to be skilled in that. I am talking of a constructive capacity to prove oneself wrong, a seminal capacity for learning and for other creative activity. And even though some students may seem to arrive with a well-established capacity to prove themselves wrong, I have also found it risky to assume that this capacity will be brought automatically into play in their activities with me.

It may be that my students are particularly hesitant to prove themselves wrong in my presence because they find me particularly fearsome. I myself don't regard myself particularly fearsome. But I know that Ghengis Khan may not have regarded himself particularly fearsome. Besides, even if I'm right in thinking I don't score more than three or four on the fearsome scale, that reassuringly low score doesn't tell much since any teacher can appear remarkably fearsome when seen from the vantage point of any student, even a student who looks calm, cool, and collected, or disconcertingly apathetic.

Accordingly, I now try to do more consistently what I did unwittingly with the colorful sister and her lineful brother. I try to help my students to advance their hidden questions about what is right and what is wrong. I try to help them to advance their hidden questions about ways to establish their rights to be wrong and therefore, their abilities to be comfortably wrong. And I try to help them to advance their hidden questions about ways to prove themselves wrong. All of which assistance I can bring myself only occasionally to offer because doing so tends to advance, and depends on advancing, my own corresponding hidden questions; and I am only occasionally up for that.

Still, when I am able to advance corresponding hidden questions that beset me when I labor in the fields in which my students are then laboring, I try to respond to their hidden questions in that indirect light. And when I can advance my questions and can recognize both similarities and differences between my students' hidden questions and mine, that helps me sometimes to curb my inclinations to encourage students to blind imitations of the ways in which I think I do things right. Which helps me sometimes to send in fewer plays from the sidelines, sometimes to suggest plays better suited to my students, and sometimes to give my students more room to run options better suited to themselves and their patients. Which helps sometimes to expose fewer patients to the terrifying experience of finding that their analyst—my student—has turned abruptly into someone else.

All of which sometimes spares me the embarrassment of teaching as if I didn't know my purples from my greens and helps me to bear it a trifle more comfortably when I don't.

More Reflections on the Nature of Hidden Questions

When I was setting out to study abnormal psychology—so called, I suppose, to wall neatly if implausibly the abnormal from the normal—the professor, perhaps in keeping with that walling intention, began the first session by saying, "Park your troubles at the door." At the time, I thought that an odd thing to say. Now I think it odder.

First I thought this was his way of telling us to relax. When I knew him better, I thought he was telling us not to. Either way, I thought he was warning us against psychobabbling about our own troubles instead of the troubles of others. Fortunately, whatever his intention, we students paid no attention. Even if there had been enough parking space and even if we had been willing and able to park our troubles at the door, I feel certain that such parking would not have been desirable for his teaching or our learning since in my opinion it's impossible for students to park their troubles at the door without parking a large part of their passion to learn.

The key connection, I believe, between trouble and learning is rooted in the duplicitous nature of hidden questions. Hidden questions address "academic" particulars of the field the hidden-question-pursuer is addressing, and hidden questions simultaneously address particulars of that person's troubles. Accordingly, the advance of these double-dealing questions is important both to the question-pursuer's "academic" and "personal" growth and development.

Unfortunately, by accepting in this way the conventional linguistic separation of the "personal" and the "academic" while trying to assert their inseparability, I may simply be obscuring the unity of the "personal" and the "academic" and may be making the inseparable seem separable. Still, linguistic limitations notwithstanding, I do not believe the "academic" and the "personal" are in actuality separable. Nor do I believe it is useful, urgent exceptions notwithstanding, to take teaching measures to make them appear separable. To the contrary, I have found consistently that gainfully employed students and teachers pursue hidden questions that, seen one way, appear academic and, seen another, appear personal.

Psychologists, particularly teachers of psychology, are always discovering what other persons already know. We like to assume it's because we're careful workers. But it may be because we're slow learners. Whatever the reason, it has taken me many years of teaching to appreciate that when the Bard called *all* the world a stage, he meant to include the classroom. Which hard-won appreciation, I believe, has helped me finally to begin to develop a clearer double vision.

Take Dr. A. In whatever "academic" matters he was bent on studying in the field before us, he consistently found ways to pursue the "personal" gentle–tough questions he was consistently bent on pursuing. I feel confident that he would have found ways in other fields to pursue with equal skill those pressing "personal" questions. That is, I feel confident he would have done so if sufficiently involved in those fields and if those fields provided—is there a field that does not?—a playground for the hidden gentle–tough questions he was so eager to pursue. If he had been deeply involved in painting, for example, I imagine he might have questioned whether to be restrained or forceful in his brushwork, timid or bold in his choice of hue and tone, delicate or firm in the delineation of form, shadowy or sharp in the use of contrast, shocking or soothing in the choice of subject, and he might have questioned whether to do many other "academic" things while exploring simultaneously his "personal" choices between the gentle and the tough.

I have repeatedly found students pursuing their ingeniously doubly turned hidden questions in surrounds I would never have suspected of harboring such grand opportunities for such pursuits. And insofar as I have sometimes inadvertently viewed the "academic" and the "personal" as separable, the "academic" has frequently turned out to be more "personal" than the "personal," and the "personal" more "academic" than the "academic."

I remember one student who played a remarkable range of tunes on one or two strings. He was a student, but not my student. He was my patient. I saw him first when, between his adolescence and early manhood, he was officially studying history though his heart was in the extracurricular study of carpentry. For a conference on the depth of what we usually call surface—we discuss very strange matters in my profession—I once wrote:

"In his associative drift, he went on day after day in reality-bound dreams and other references to household repairs. Nothing seemed addressable till I grasped at last that he was passionately involved in an extraordinary range of (hidden) questions about how to attach one thing to another: whether by adhesive or nail or screw, whether by joinings that adhere the parts tightly or loosely, whether by dove-tailing or simpler abutting, whether temporarily or more permanently, whether by this or that reversible or relatively irreversible means. It's remarkable how large a world can be joined—passionately joined—to the seemingly small world of joinery. I imagine you can imagine the range of (inner) questions then salient. But I imagine you cannot imagine how often and how assiduously he pursued these and other inquiries, in the metaphors we usually call metaphor and in those we usually call actuality, using the dialects of carpentry."

Over and over, I found this young man pursuing a few joinery questions in his "outer" world of carpentry in harmony with many "inner" world questions of other forms of joinery. But if he had hired me to help him to explore carpentry rather than his psyche, I imagine I would have found him pursuing a few inner-world joinery questions in harmony with many outer-world carpentry questions regarding the best ways to join one material and another.

More than a decade later, when he had moved from the avocation of carpentry to the vocation of architecture and had come back to tell me of his progress, I was impressed by the many ways he now found in architecture to advance old and new hidden questions about old and new joinings, hidden questions cannily crafted concurrently to explore old and new joinings of his "inner" and "outer" worlds.

Similar double agendas of inquiry advanced by other students in other circumstances have led me to these assumptions:

1) Where a student's hidden questions bridge most conspicuously between the "personal" and the "academic," a student's heart and head can, to the degree they sometimes can, best join.

2) Where a teacher's hidden questions bridge most conspicuously between the "personal" and the "academic," a teacher's heart and head can, to the degree they sometimes can, best join.

3) Where a student's liveliest hidden questions and a teacher's hidden questions can best seek and find correspondence is where learning and teaching can, to the degree they sometimes can, best join.

Which mix of assumptions and observations has made me more and more skeptical that students or teachers can long park their troubles at the door without becoming lackadaisical.

Once More Backward

Today's journal is full of yesterday, and yesterday's is full of today. Which is not always apparent till yesterday has become today. I have mentioned before that somewhere along the teaching way I recalled my third-grade complaint that my teachers always taught what they wanted to teach and never what I wanted to learn. But I failed to mention how I happened to remember.

One night, having written in my journal of a fruitless effort that day to teach in accord with a student's hidden question, I dreamed I was writing with a stylus. When I awoke, my thoughts went quickly to the woes of stylus writing and then to the teaching woes of the previous day. Which was when I was carried back to the third grade, where I had struggled to write with one of those steel-tipped pens we dipped in those little corner-of-the-desk ink wells filled each day by Allen Stypeck, who poured carefully, and never spilled much, the watery blue ink in those large bottles with the little black spigots. And it was then, having relived that historical transition from pencil to pen, that I remembered with a start that it was with one of those stylus-pens that I had written in my third-grade journal my aforementioned composition containing my complaint that my teachers always taught what they wanted to teach and never what I wanted to learn.

On the Importance of Being
a Bit Off

A mother was seated in a park with her baby when an airplane passed overhead. The little fellow shouted, "Ooh ooh. Ooh ooh." To which his mother replied, "Yes, dear. That's an airplane."

I read about this event in a reputable professional journal. I propose, therefore, to take it as true.

I once reported the event to a fellow teacher. He was not impressed. He said that whether or not the story was true, it did not, as I had suggested, provide a relevant instance of teaching in accord with hidden questions. If I remember his exact words, he said, "If you mean this to be an example of teaching in accord with hidden questions, it simply won't fly." I told the story to another teacher. She said I was blurring the distinction between a homunculus theory and an epigenetic theory. I told it to still another, who underscored the importance of the nature–nurture controversy and its bearing on our efforts to understand an infant's acquisition of language. I turned at last to a teacher in my own field. He informed me that learning the difference between an "ooh ooh" and an "airplane" is not comparable to learning to become a psychoanalyst, since learning language comes naturally and learning to become a psychoanalyst definitely does not.

Despite these weighty warnings, I cannot stop thinking about that mother's efforts to teach her son and the sizeable problems she faced. It seems clear that she was trying to affirm her son's enthusiastic efforts to talk and trying to offer a suggestion about how he might refer more expeditiously to the overhead vehicle for whose name she surmised he was reaching. But it also seems clear that this well-intentioned mother could not possibly have been sure that "ooh ooh" was really a reference to the airplane. And even if she could, how could she have been sure whether "ooh ooh" reflected her son's effort to name the overhead object, his delight with its speed, his joyful imitation of its sound, his dismay at its departure, his complaint about its loudness, his cry of apprehension about its size, its speed, or its vibrations, a magical effort to master an auditory invasion through imitation, or perhaps a nonjudgmental acknowledgment of whatever he had heard, felt, or seen?

Given that wide range of possibilities, she might understandably have chosen to hang back and await further clues. But she seems readily to have understood that by definition her job was to press on. Accordingly, relying heavily on intuition, as any true teacher must, she responded rapidly as if her baby had without question been pursuing hidden questions about the terminology he might employ to designate appropriately the object he had temporarily called an "ooh ooh." And, responding to that almost-but-not-quite asked question of taxonomy, she seized gracefully the opportunity to teach him that a synonym for "ooh ooh" is "airplane."

What person would declare this bad teaching? Would anyone but a fanatic for objectivity insist that the subtleties of "ooh ooh" are too large to be caught by the term "airplane"? Even a stickler for accuracy would be forced to concede that no word catches all the subtleties of anything. Who would suggest that in the light of the inevitable limitations of language the mother should have stopped talking? Wouldn't the little fellow then also be likely to stop?

I don't pretend to be able to assess the adequacy of this mother's teaching. But I feel moved to assert that if she never talked as if she were sure of what her son was trying to say, and if she never talked surely when she couldn't possibly be sure, that would surely not be good for her son, for herself, or for the many others with whom her son must try tomorrow to converse.

Granting that the little fellow's "ooh ooh" may have meant "gone, gone" or "uh-oh" or "aha" or "no, no," or something else, who can fault his mother for assuming that "ooh ooh" was onomatopoesical for the aeronautical? Besides, even if she was mistaken in her assumption that her son was pursuing hidden questions about the proper name of the object to which she assumed he was referring, and even if her son ended this particular encounter thinking "airplane" means "gone, gone," or "uh-oh," or "aha," or "no, no"—or who knows what else— what's the great harm? Cannot subsequent lessons be expected to set things straight? Who would deny that teaching anyone anything by any means is largely a matter of teaching something that will later need to be straightened out? For that matter, is there anyone who has reached adulthood without having to straighten out many things—perhaps all—that his or her parents taught him or her in childhood? Who can go on living consistently with such homilies as, "It's better to give than to receive"? And who can go on taking seriously such contradictory homilies as, "He who hesitates is lost" and "Look before you leap"?

Furthermore, suppose the situation had been reversed. Suppose the little fellow had said, "airplane" and his mother had said, "Yes, dear, that's an ooh ooh." Is there a teacher who has never done that? Besides, suppose, improbable as it may seem, this mother were able always to guess rightly what her son was asking cryptically. Would such bliss be a blessing for learning? With harmony like that, what little one or large would ever pay attention to problems of terminology or find cause to spring for autonomy?

As for the question of what is learned naturally and what is not, that's a natural but unanswerable question. It may be natural to learn. It may be natural to learn to talk. It may be natural to begin with a natural range of sounds and, with the help of nurture, natural to forge them into commonly acceptable natural and unnatural sounds. But would anyone maintain there's anything natural about learning to say "airplane" instead of "ooh ooh"? Would anyone claim that any person of sound mind would choose "airplane" over "ooh ooh" entirely on his or her own?

I see no reason to doubt that even the most elementary grasp of the most elementary subject, and the most advanced pursuit of the most advanced, involve the learning of some things that come naturally and some that do not. Moreover, it seems entirely natural to me to conclude that for both the learning of the natural and the learning of the un, and for endless mixes of the two, an encouraging (small) delusion — a mother's, father's or other true teacher's — about the nature of a student's hidden questions is seldom a calamity and usually a galvanic necessity.

Who in the world would trade "ooh oohs" for "airplanes" without a teacher who believes, is delighted to believe, and is more than a little mistaken to believe that the ooh-ooh sayer is almost but not quite asking how to say airplane? Who would learn to walk, or at least learn as readily, without the delight of an intimate observer who believes that the one about to walk is already wondering how to walk, already struggling to walk, and, what's more, when at last staggering, is already walking?

In my opinion, it deserves wider recognition that any teacher — whether mother, father, or other, and especially one who proposes to teach in accord with hidden questions — can ill afford to underestimate the importance of being a bit off. How fortunate, therefore, that teaching in accord with hidden questions affords so many large and significant opportunities to be at least a little bit off.

On Trying to Teach
in Large Groups as Well as
Small, or Almost as Well

Because hidden questions promise answers to distressing problems, they appeal. Because hidden questions threaten to en-
lighten specters we prefer to darken, they pester. Accordingly,
when hidden questions call, it's no surprise that we try both to
welcome and to hang up on the callers.

Mixed responses to hidden questions are readily observable in one-on-one learning and teaching. And they are even
more readily observable in large-group learning and teaching.
By large group I refer to any group larger than one-on-one. In
many fields, they call one-on-one, tutorial. In mine, in appreciation of its pleasing connotation that the teacher observes
things from on high, we call one-on-one, supervision. For
present purposes, however, I have decided to forgo that
pleasure and to refer, on one hand, to one-on-one, and, on the
other, to larger than one-on-one, or simply, large.

The reader might wonder why I have spoken so much of

the one-on-one and so little of the large. The reader might also wonder whether anything I have said about the one-on-one has any relevance to the large learning and teaching situations in which most teachers are mainly or entirely involved. Indeed, I showed this book—this manuscript moving toward a book —to a friend who showed it to his wife, who is a teacher in training. And he reported back that she said she did not see how anything I had said about teaching—either about teaching in accord with hidden questions or other—could help her to teach Latin to the students she was soon to teach.

I have the impression that this budding teacher may have been expecting to teach rather large groups of rather less than eager students. If so, I can readily understand that she might find it hard to imagine tracking hidden questions in those circumstances. And even if she could anticipate being able to track students' hidden questions, she might understandably wonder how being aware of those questions could help her to help her students to devote themselves to the drilling necessary to gain a mastery of Latin vocabulary, declension, and conjugation. Nevertheless, though I can appreciate the possible complexities of her circumstances and the unquestionable complexities of the subject to be taught, I am tempted, in reply to her almost-asked question about how teaching in accord with students' hidden questions might help her to teach Latin, merely to assert that teaching in accord with hidden questions might prove to be just what is necessary to avoid making Latin a dead language.

But such an assertion about the possibility of rescuing Latin from its usual fate—even if that assertion may be correct—cannot conceal that I know entirely too little of this teacher, of the circumstances in which she is to teach, of her students, and of Latin vocabulary, declension, and conjugation to meet the challenge of providing an illustration of how teaching in accord with hidden questions might help her to advance the teaching and learning of Latin. The unfortunate fact is that although I suspect that many students, given the right materials and climate, could manage to bridge between their inner and outer worlds and the ancient worlds of Roman morality, sexuality, freedom and slavery, law and order, war and peace, militarism, public spectacles, amphitheaters, aqueducts, atria, and the like, and though I suspect that playing between such connections and the teaching and learning of Latin might offer a sizeable advantage over daily making and breaking camp with Caesar, I cannot say precisely, or even roughly, how. Rather, I must content myself with expressing a cautious faith that a teacher who knows her subject and her students well-enough and who addresses the problem creatively is likely to find good-enough ways to help students to bridge between their hidden questions and even so unlikely a task as the learning of the rudiments of Latin.

Though unable to offer particulars, I would nevertheless like to offer a few general observations about the expectable difficulties of tracking and teaching in accord with hidden questions in large groups. Whether these observations can prove helpful to a teacher of Latin, a teacher of another subject, or even to another teacher in my own field remains to be seen.

Having first tracked hidden questions one-on-one, I tried soon after to apply that orientation to groups larger than one-on-one and learned that I could not. That is, I learned that at first I could not.

I found myself confronting a number of interlocking problems. I found that the larger the group, the fewer the hidden questions. I found that when large groups were confronted with even a few hidden questions, they acted speedily to squelch them. I found large groups more adept at hiding questions behind questionable answers than at uncovering the questions hidden behind questionable answers. I found persons with prepared answers more numerous and outspoken in large groups than persons with almost-but-not-quite-asked questions. I found large groups more frightened than heartened by hidden questions, more inclined to prize overt answers than hidden questions, and, even when showing a grudging tolerance, more tolerant of ailing questions than of sturdy. And having observed these and other vexing obstacles to teaching in accord with hidden questions in large groups, I took my findings to confirm the old saw: "A mule is a horse put together by a committee." Accordingly, I concluded that the sole way to teach in accord with hidden questions is to teach one-on-one. I have, however, since changed my mind.

Granted that large groups often seem wary of hidden questions. Granted that distractions in large groups may make it difficult to pay attention to hidden questions. And granted that hidden questions in large groups may sometimes seem to fly off in such diverse directions that it becomes difficult to pay attention to those questions and even harder to know which questions to address.

Still, despite these initial difficulties, I have since found that teaching in accord with hidden questions in large groups frequently goes reasonably well. (I imagine that most teachers will agree that, in teaching, nothing ever goes better than reasonably well.) But even slight advances in my capacity to teach in accord with hidden questions in large groups have required that I confront more than one problem in my approach.

I found early on that I was paying too much attention to the easily identifiable hidden questions of a few individuals and too little attention to the hidden questions emerging in common. (In referring to questions emerging in common, or to group questions, I don't mean to suggest an unconscious, Durkheimian group consciousness, but rather an emerging synergy of some hidden questions of some individuals in the group.) And I found that when I could tune and respond to group questions, the individual questions began to consolidate and to become clearer. Which made it easier to tune and to respond to individual hidden questions in ways that sometimes helped them to converge and sometimes helped to reveal that they had all along been less divergent than they had at first seemed. In turn, that apparent increased harmony of individual questions made it somewhat easier to keep track of and respond to them in ways that assisted the advance of group questions. In short, I found things went better when I could shift my attention back and forth between seemingly insular hidden questions of individuals and questions emerging in common, provided that in the midst of that shifting I paid predominant attention to the questions emerging in common.

In time, I also found, and still find, that an even larger obstacle than my angle of vision lies in my persistent inclinations to disrupt the advance of hidden questions in large groups. And though I had already become aware of such inclinations when teaching one-on-one, I found them accentuated in large groups, accentuated, I believe, both by the larger number of hidden questions threatening my equanimity and by the larger number of individuals eager to collude with my inclinations to disrupt.

I have learned that I have many ingenious ways of neglecting, obstructing, obscuring, and eliminating hidden questions in large groups. And I have learned that I am adept at using many existing forms of large-group teaching for the purpose of disrupting hidden questions, which utilization takes no great skill since so many forms of large-group teaching seem to have been perfected precisely with that end in mind. For example:

Almost a century ago in centers of medicine the case conference was invented and raised soon after to its now eminent pedagogical position. Nor was it long before the case conference was used and in some ways improved in centers of law and then of business. But through all these developments, and however different in some particulars, case conferences have shared and still share many characteristics in common.

In a well-run case conference, tradition requires that as much data as possible be gathered in advance as carefully as possible by a designated data gatherer. At a designated time that designated person presents that data to as many persons as possible as hurriedly as possible in halls built as large as possible, and preferably amphitheatrical. After which, a designated big hitter steps forth and, rapidly adding, subtracting, dividing, multiplying, and abstracting the previously presented pieces, arrives at a dazzling sum; to which she or he customarily adds a prediction of events to come, or at least a postdiction of events past, to which she or he has not previously been made privy.

After these crowning predictions or postdictions have been advanced, other participants are encouraged to perform similar feats of cerebration till at last still another designated person brings forth a few key facts known right along by that person but withheld from the others. When those facts have been presented, they generally affirm abundantly the wisdom of some participants, usually one though sometimes none, and the folly of others, sometimes one but usually many.

These exercises are often highly entertaining, impart useful information, sharpen quickness of mind, and offer large opportunities for competition, exhibition, and pontification. Unfortunately, however, the ways in which conclusions are reached in case conferences are generally sharply at odds with the more trial-and-error-ish ways in which workers actually work when they work in the field whose workings these conferences are ostensibly concerned with advancing. Which might not seem a problem except that after long exposure to case conference doings, the participants—students and teachers alike—often begin to think and act outside conferences as if inside. The net result of which is that case conferences, both in their immediate and long-term effects, often prove considerably less salutary for advancing hidden questions than for disrupting.

I don't mean to suggest that case conferences or other forms of large-group teaching are responsible for the troubles I have experienced in tracking and teaching in accord with students' hidden questions. I mean, rather, to report that I have found that large groups provide conditions highly supportive of my students' and my propensities to avoid or to disrupt hidden questions, our own and each other's. And I have found that teaching in accord with hidden questions in large groups of whatever form has required an even more vigilant and persistent monitoring of my ways and reasons for disrupting the advance of hidden questions than has one-on-one teaching.

Therefore, insofar as large-group teaching stirs me repeatedly and provides me many opportunities to disrupt the advance of hidden questions, it has helped me to learn a little more about the ways and reasons I do so in groups large and small. Which has strengthened my conviction that teaching in accord with hidden questions is largely a matter of turning problems to occasional advantage. And since many problems are compounded in large groups, large-group teaching offers many opportunities to turn problems to occasional advantage.

Accordingly, when recommending teaching in accord with hidden questions I do not find it necessary to urge a return to the golden days of one student and one teacher on a log. I am content to say that a little less large-group teaching, without large loss to anyone, might free a few more teachers for a little more one-on-one teaching. Which might not be a bad thing for students or teachers. Students might benefit directly from the increase of one-on-one insofar as it helps them to advance their hidden questions; and they might benefit as well as from the consequent improvements in their participation in the larger than one-on one, especially from their heightened capacity to advance hidden questions in the larger. And teachers might learn something from tracking and teaching in accord with hidden questions in the one-on-one that might help them to track and teach in accord with hidden questions in both the one-on-one and the larger. Another reason I no longer feel inclined to minimize the possibilities of teaching in accord with hidden questions in large groups is that I have come to the view that some hidden questions are better advanced one-on-one and some in large groups. That is, I have come to the view that for teaching in accord with hidden questions, as for teaching in accord with other visions, one-on-one is better for some purposes and large group for others. And I have high hopes that someday someone might learn something about which is better for which.

All in all, I have found that teaching in accord with hidden questions, whether in large groups or small, is helpful both for teaching and for learning a little of what goes on in learning and teaching. Which is why I have stuck with large group teaching as well as small. Which is also why, despite a slim knowledge of Latin, and an even slimmer knowledge of the rigors of teaching it, I dare to keep wondering whether teaching in accord with hidden questions in large groups or small might in some way or other prove useful to a teacher and a student of Latin.

On Finding Three-Ring
Circuses
and on Other Merits of
Tending to Hidden Questions

I have watched myself and other teachers trying to teach. I have watched students trying to learn. I have psychoanalyzed students and teachers. I have talked with teachers at nearby institutions of learning, with teachers across the nearby river, and with teachers in other parts of this country and of several countries abroad. I have talked with teachers in my field and teachers in others and teachers who teach small and large students in small and large groups. I have read newspapers, magazines, journals, and books and attended as many academic gatherings as I could abide. I have concluded from these experiences that modern teachers, like ancient Greek and later Catechistic, and like the followers of Erasmus, Rousseau, Dewey, Whitehead, Lord Ashby, Ortega, and many between and since, are divisible in toto, as Gaul was, in three.

Some teachers say our job is to impart knowledge and the love of knowledge. They say students today are too ready to seek practical uses for knowledge they have barely grasped and too ready to shun studies whose value escapes their immediate appreciation. They say students' deficiencies of patience and perseverance are growing larger and their attention spans shorter. They say students watch television too much, read too little, and even when they read enough, read the wrong things, and even when they read the right things, read them for the wrong reasons. They say students are becoming increasingly high on action, low on contemplation, and full of misguided pragmatism. They regard all this the legacy of a technological world run wild.

Other teachers says we must bring our teaching down to earth. They say knowledge is not knowledge unless it makes a knowledgeable difference. They say we must teach practical facts and the practical uses of practical facts. They say students today come overloaded with trivial information and are eager for more and that their growing appetite for the trivial is met and wetted, though never satiated, by television's ever-quickening transmission of useless information passed along by an ever-expanding cadre of commentators chosen mainly for their looks and with little or no regard for their abilities to sift the gold from the gravel. They say our first and foremost task, therefore, is to impart to our students a proper respect for ideas of practical consequence for humankind and its surround.

A third group has it that we must help our students to look to the heavens or other uplifted and uplifting events. They say students today know too much of rock and too little of the Rock of Ages. They say students today lack the gyroscopic action of moral vision and, accordingly, unless helped appropriately, are doomed to gyrate aimlessly and endlessly. They say students are mired in empty relativism, rarely know the great myths of our culture, and, if they do, see only the dated denotations and fail to see the timeless connotations and are doomed therefore to try desperately and fruitlessly to fill with drugs, sex, and material goods, vacuums that are moral and therefore unfillable by these ill-chosen means. These teachers say we must impart to our students a knowledge and a love of the great moral truths to be grasped from discriminating readings of Plato, the Bible (St. James version), Shakespeare, and other great works that have stood the test of time and of great teachers. There are tribal disputes among these teachers about which great moral truths to teach and which great works to assign, but there is solid agreement that great moral truth must persistently be taught.

Though these three groups of teachers differ in some respects—one touting the imparting of knowledge for its beauty, one for its utility, and one for its morality—they are all of the same genus. They share the conviction that things are not what they used to be. They agree on the necessity of "imparting" whatever needs imparting. And when teaching, and not merely talking about teaching, in spite of their differences of emphasis they all seem to help their students to learn facts, to learn the useful applications of facts, and to learn to place some facts and their utility under moral scrutiny.

Moreover, whatever their differences, teachers of all three groups seem frequently to teach, willy nilly, what their students are trying knowingly or unknowingly to learn and toward which their hidden questions are repeatedly addressed: knowledge for its beauty, knowledge for its utility, and knowledge to be placed under, and in the service of advancing, morality. (By morality, or better still, moral scrutiny, I do not refer to any particular brand but rather to diverse religious and irreligious struggles to find visions and ways to advance the mutual welfare of self and other.) I have found that when learning and teaching go particularly well, hidden questions about beauties, utilities, and moralities repeatedly advance, meet, and join in Whiteheadian rhythms of romance, precision, and generalization. And those laudable festivities have heightened my impression that teaching in tune with students' hidden questions is not without merit.

To put diagrammatically and cross-sectionally this spirited play of hidden questions within and among the aforementioned spheres, I borrow the following representation from set theory (not to be confused with beer ads or Olympic emblems):

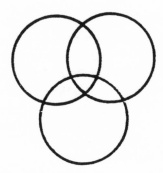

And now, hoping to reach a conclusion somewhere between a whimper and a bang, I want to set down the impression that when things have gone well, teaching and learning in accord with hidden questions have (sometimes) helped my students and me:

1. to advance our hidden questions;
2. to advance our capacities to advance hidden questions;
3. to advance correspondences between our hidden questions;
4. to learn facts and theories of the field before us;
5. to extend our abilities to use the tools of observation of the field before us;
6. to question a few facts, theories, and tools of that field; and
7. to expand our rights to be wrong.

What's more, teaching in accord with hidden questions has (sometimes) helped me:

1. to learn more about those I have tried to teach;
2. to temper my furors to teach;
3. to indulge while teaching in "serious play";
4. to study that play within and between learning and teaching, and within and between my students and me;
5. to observe and modify my ways and motives for interfering with the teaching and learning I purport to be advancing; and has even helped me (on occasion)

6. to find something interesting about teaching on days
   when teaching has been less than a pure delight.

It is in the light of these substantial, if only occasional,
advantages that I cautiously recommend trying to teach in
accord with hidden questions. That is, I cautiously recommend
that activity to anyone rash enough to try to teach by any
means whatsoever anything whatsoever to anyone whomso-
ever. And realizing that few true teachers would be moved by
empirical considerations unaccompanied by theoretical, I want
now to relocate my assumptions in a brief rationale. For the
sake of brevity, I state those assumptions and rationale cate-
gorically:

Human development, whether "personal," "academic,"
psychological, physical, political or other, occurs characteristically in progressive bursts separated by relatively longer
stretches of relatively slower change. On the verge of such
bursts, individuals or groups become a trifle unhinged and
return to earlier challenges, dilemmas, and solutions until, in
transcendental leaps, they can bring old solutions to new and
better conclusions. In these moments of wobbling before
leaping, the liveliest hidden questions, sparked by the resur-
gence of old tensions and shaped by the current play of inner
and outer worlds, press even more importunately than usual
for expression. And it is these moments of inquisitive hesitation that mark the largest opportunities for learning and
teaching.

In trying to arrive at a simplifying conclusion, have I
reified the highly fluid operations that constitute hidden questions? Have I conjured images of questions lurking full blown
in students' heads? Have I blurred the picture I meant to
convey of incipient questions, proto-questions, inclinations to
questions, the stuff of which questions are made? Have I given
the impression that I consider my perceptions of students'
hidden questions to be free of my own subjectivities? Have I
slid into a naive idealism? Am I mired in a romantic fallacy?

I can only resay what I have meant to say. I have found
repeatedly that my hidden questions and assumptions, espe-

cially my assumptions about what constitutes a useful question, shape persistently how I perceive, how I join, and how I influence the unfolding of what I infer to be my students' incipient hidden questions; and what I infer to be my students' incipient hidden questions shape persistently what I infer to be my own. And on and on. I have found too that a persistent scrutiny of my subjectivities is necessary in order to render them relatively informed subjectivities that facilitate, to the degree possible, exchanges that advance my students' hidden questions and my own and that facilitate, to the degree possible, discoveries that reveal some of the ways in which the one has helped to advance the other and some of the ways in which the one has helped to obstruct the other.

Furthermore, I don't mean to suggest that my students' hidden questions and my own are, or if unobstructed would be, pure expressions of our best learning and teaching inclinations. To the contrary, I have found repeatedly that my students' and my hidden questions, like our responses to them, are elaborate expressions of our inclinations both to advance and to obstruct learning. Indeed, I have found it useful to assume that my students and I are always trying both to advance and to obstruct learning and teaching. And I have found that trying to track hidden questions helps me to pay more careful attention to both positive and negative inclinations and, here and there, to get into better position to accentuate the positive. Whether other teachers and students, including those who teach and learn subjects seemingly less loaded, are equally likely to be working so persistently at cross purposes, is a question I can only raise and only others can answer.

Afterword: Studenthood

Having said a few things about my experiences as a teacher, I want now to say a few things about my experiences as a student. The high point of the latter may have come on my first day of school. The setting was not a fabled little red school-house but one of those lofty latter-day Gothic edifices considered in the thirties the most fitting setting for elementary school teaching in Flatbush in the Borough of Brooklyn in the City of New York. In that grand grey building, at the start of each day, we students of all classes of all eight grades lined up in the basement as well as we could, which was never particularly, and subsequently, after a long wait, at the sound of a loud bell—or when the bell failed, a shrill whistle—we marched briskly forward and upward to our classrooms.

In the face of those long waits and forced marches, we never flinched. In those golden-rule days, we were a hardy lot. We never eased into first grade by way of nursery school, prekindergarten, kindergarten, or other soft touches. And we were never bussed or carred to school. Through fair weather and foul, we walked. And even when arriving for the first day of school, we waited patiently in the basement, then marched confidently forward and upward, and got down at once to first-class business.

And that's where wee Willie MacMullen came in. And where he yearned to get out. After little more than an hour of that first class, Willie MacMullen, who sat as far up front as anyone could sit—where no other student on that or any succeeding day ever chose to sit—raised his hand high and kept it there till Miss Strom asked what he wanted. Willie Mac-Mullen rose smartly from his seat, as we had already been taught to rise, and standing as tall as he could, which was not very, wee Willie, in the clear and measured cadences of a child who had spoken more with adults than with children, announced without hesitation:

"I don't like it here. If you'll take me across Glenwood Road, I'll go home now."

For a long and breathless moment, we thirty-odd students sat in a fidgetless silence. Which was extremely rare even in P. S. 152, where silence in the classroom was assiduously pre-scribed and fidgeting assiduously proscribed. We were stunned. We could understand that Willie MacMullen did not like school. But we couldn't imagine anyone saying it out loud. And we couldn't imagine anyone saying that he wanted—which meant he needed—to go home. Besides, we found it incomprehensible that anyone would admit needing help in crossing Glenwood Road, even if he or she had been advised by ill-advised parents to seek help in crossing.

What I remember best and most fondly is that in the face of Willie MacMullen's shocking revelation, Miss Strom re-mained nonplussed. A thing like that is hard to forget. She looked at Willie with an angelic smile and then, after a very brief pause, complimented him warmly for the politeness and the clarity with which he had spoken; after which, she ex-pressed regret that unfortunately she could not comply with Willie's well-spoken request. Right then and there I fell in love with Miss Strom. Well perhaps not right then and there, but not long after.

Miss Strom was a remarkable person, especially in P. S. 152. Miss Strom was sweet, gentle, and pretty. But it was not solely her sweetness, gentility, or beauty that caught my attention and earned my abiding affection. Probably I could not have said it at the time, but retrospectively I can see clearly that what captivated me most especially was Miss Strom's unflagging determination and ability to find the best in students under the most trying circumstances. Which lesson from Miss Strom was far and away the best lesson I ever received about teaching.

In P. S. 152 we pupils—we were always called pupils, which I found quite puzzling since I had learned by then that the pupil was the hole in the center of the eye—distinguished carefully between teachers who were "nice" and teachers who were "mean." And by our careful count we established confidently that the "nice" were far outnumbered by the "mean." Nor was I alone in my belief that Miss Strom ranked high among the nice. Moreover, to this day, I have not met a single person who professed to believe otherwise.

Miss Strom was a princess, of which they did not make many, spreading sweetness and light in that grey Gothic school by the side of Glenwood Road. And the fortuitous fit between Miss Strom's accommodative personality and Willie MacMullen's aversive, stirred me to a lifelong interest in the myriad fits and misfits of accommodative, assertive, and aversive students and accommodative, assertive, and aversive teachers.

Not long after, I learned that my love for Miss Strom had not been misplaced. She made me a bank monitor. And shortly after that, she saw to it that I was placed in Rapid Advance. Those thoughtful decisions have since proved clear signs of Miss Strom's perspicacity. From that time on, I have stayed out of some mischief and gotten into other by playing the part of a monitor. And though Rapid Advance may sound to the uninitiated like the name of a public transit system, that placement got me off to a very fast start and provided my first and richest taste of life in the fast lane.

Nor did these exhilarating encounters with Miss Strom

end there. Six years later, when she had become Mrs. Phelps, she was again my teacher. This time, however, I did not find her so congenial. And her smile now seemed not so much pretty as syrupy. Which got me, now eleven going on twelve, to wondering whether Miss Strom, now Mrs. Phelps, had changed, or I.

Most of all, what Miss Strom taught me the first time round was that even in conduct beyond the pale—and Willie MacMullen's was surely that—there are almost always praise-worthy possibilities. And what Mrs. Phelps taught me to ponder the second time round is the impact of the observer's state on what the observer observes, and, in particular, the impact of changes in the observer on what the observer observes to be changes in the observed. Accordingly, though Miss Strom was officially helping me to read Dickie Dare and Mrs. Phelps, to read American History, I have concluded that what she—they—were teaching most cogently were visions first of possibility and next, of relativity. And to this day I marvel at the wisdom it took for Mr. Beisheim, the principal of P. S. 152, to have said "Let's put this little boy of six in with this sweet unmarried teacher in her mid-twenties and then later, when he is eleven going on twelve and she a trifle past thirty and newly wed, let's put them together again and see what teaching and learning is happening."

If Miss Strom stands out as "nice," Miss Murphy stands out as "mean." Miss Murphy was our gym teacher. As much as Ms. Strom-Phelps was accommodative, Miss Murphy was assertive. And Miss Murphy had a remarkable right arm. I know because Miss Murphy led us in calisthenics and if anyone was slack in that pursuit, she would grab with her left hand the whistle she always wore round her neck, blow an ear-splitting signal that something was terribly amiss—the same whistle that sometimes got us started at the beginning of the day when the bell failed—simultaneously bring her right arm round and down in an uninterrupted backward circle, and then as that remarkable arm came forward, release the basketball she always held and direct it at the startled culprit with uncanny accuracy.

Miss Murphy always knew exactly what we were doing.

Her right hand always knew exactly what her left hand was doing. And the sound of her warning whistle never preceded by more than a fraction of a second the arrival of the right- hand thrown ball. In all the years since, I have never seen anyone who could match Miss Murphy's peripheral vision or ballistic concision, with the possible exception of Bob Cousy, who, with a similar windmill motion, would throw, though without the accompanying whistle, his now fabled full-court pass. I do not know with certainty what Miss Murphy thought she was teaching. But I do know that her awesome propulsive feats taught me lessons in precision, stirred me to great heights of calisthenic ambition, and heightened my fascination with edge-of-awareness perception. What's more, her athletic attitudes and activities engendered in me a lifelong respect for unexpected possibilities. Considerably before I ever heard women's rights and capabilities properly pressed, assessed, or discussed, Miss Murphy shattered my prior conviction that girls lacked the ability to throw a ball properly. And in so doing, she made me forever less certain of what both women and men can and cannot do.

Aided by such teachers, my education proceeded apace. Miss Pearson taught English Six—or perhaps English Seven— but it was actually almost entirely elocution. It wasn't Miss Pearson's accent that bothered us. All of us had heard many foreign accents. But other persons were good enough not to try to foist their accents on us, whereas Miss Pearson, who was from Chester, England, was on a holy crusade to convert our accents to "proper English." Whenever, for example, she found it necessary to say "I cahhnt understahnd you" to any one of us, she would assign to all of us remedial exercises for our flattened A's, other flattened vowels, and even our flattened diphthongs. And so she tried repeatedly to teach us how to say, roundly and unnasally, "How now brown cow!" and "Why are you bounding about the house?" and "My mother made lunch for me" and other strange sayings. Which might not have been so bad if she had not also insisted that we pronounce every word ending in a y as if it ended in an i, as, for instance, "Isn't that an extraordinarili, pretti, kitti?" Nor did it help to lessen my misgivings about this way of talking when, on trying it one day after school, I met with nothing but ridicule from my friends who had not had the advantage of Miss Pearson's teaching.

Still, I can now appreciate what I could not appreciate at the time. There was method to Miss Pearson's madness. She got me to thinking early about the importance of speaking the language of the person with whom you wish to speak. And soon after Miss Pearson tried to teach me to speak properly, I became fascinated with trying to figure out from their accents where people came from. Which led me to listen to a fellow on the radio who would ask people to say things like merry, marry, fairy, ferry, Washington, water, and daughter and would then guess their home state, often their town, and sometimes their part of town. And so, though Miss Pearson never did help me to talk as if I were British, the habits of listening she inspired made a paramount contribution to my later participation in an occupation one of whose peculiar preoccupations is divining whatever can be divined from whatever people say and fail to say and however they say and fail to say it.

Miss Dubois taught music. In Miss Dubois's class, we listened dutifully to recordings of "This is the symphony that Schubert wrote and never finished," "Caveleria Rusticana," The "Swan," and even to parts of the "Surprise Symphony," the last of which I found fair to middling but not particularly surprising. Miss Dubois taught us to listen so attentively that after hearing a remarkably few measures, we could invariably call these and other gems by their right names. And, for my part, I learned to perform this feat so well and automatically that to this day I find it hard to attend a concert without raising my hand.

Miss Dubois had an ear for music and a mind for surprise. Miss Dubois came up with the idea that at graduation we should perform the Pinafore. Which mistake might not have been so bad except that the only one among us who could sing was Paul Blum, who in assembly each Christmas sang "O Holy Night," "Adeste Fidelis," "The First Noel," "A Partridge in a

Pear Tree," "Merry Gentlemen," "Silent Night," and "Jingle Bells," and each Easter, "Ave Maria." Anyone who knew anything knew that Paul Blum was a first-rate singer; at least he was a first-rate singer before his voice started changing and not for the better. Which was why he was not available for the "Pinafore" and why many of us who had previously been happy listeners were forced suddenly and unexpectedly to become unhappy singers.

Undaunted by developments that would surely have daunted a lesser teacher, Miss Dubois chose Laura Abrams, who had blonde hair and was very cute, to play Buttercup. And Miss D. chose others for other "Pinafore" parts for other, nonmusical reasons. Mine was a case in point. Following a cursory audition requiring my singing an octave while Miss Dubois was playing it on the piano—a procedure stacked in my misfavor since I had recently learned to play the piano—I was chosen for the role of Captain, a role, that unfortunately, as I was soon to learn, requires more than an octave.

Miss Dubois may have thought she was teaching music. But I knew better. I saw at once that she was teaching perseverance in the face of unremitting agony. And after months of preparation, lunging desperately at a very small straw, I decided that if I ever got through "I Am the Captain of the Pinafore" and "Goodness Me, Why What was That?" and other songs of that ilk, which I have since forgotten, I would never again be so scared in a public performance. Which proved true. And though that may seem a small good in a line of work in which one is seldom called on for public perfor- mance, nevertheless, what I learned from Miss Dubois has come in surprisingly handy. I learned in particular how good it feels when you stop doing in the second place what you were never qualified to do, never liked to do, and never should have done in the first. And that taught me always to ponder carefully the question of when to persevere and when not to. And that helped me soon to give up playing the piano privately and singing publicly. And it helped me eventually to stop studenting and to replace it with teaching.

In Erasmus Hall High School, where I learned nothing

about Desiderius Erasmus, I learned Latin. (It's remarkable how Latin keeps coming back from the past.) And though I did not learn much, I learned how many English words sound like Latin and how many Latin words sound like English and if you know the English you can guess the Latin and vice versa; and so I went on to study more Latin in college and did not demur when the Latin teacher recruited us to take Greek so that Greek would not be dropped from the curriculum. And that proved to be an excellent decision because I have forever after been proud to have made this sizeable sacrifice to save Greece from extinction. What's more, I learned from a Bible student in that class how important it is to determine whether a particular Greek word means "with" or "into" since that determines whether baptism should be done by sprinkling a person with "water" or plunging him or her "into." And I also learned that thalassa, which some people call thalata, means the sea, and that the thalassa people and the thalata people rarely see eye to eye and sometimes go at their differences toe to toe. And so, though I never learned much Latin or Greek, I did learn from these classical studies that small matters can have singularly large consequences, that one small thing can lead to another and another, and that you never know where a little teaching and learning may lead, all of which proved extremely useful when I later gave up being a student and became a teacher.

Mr. Correra taught civics. For Mr. Correra, we read the New York Times every day and came in ready to say how the writers had tried, through many tricks of journalism, to misguide the unwary reader. And Mr. Correra would say every day, "Well, what 'usually reliable source' has said what usual nonsense today?" "Did the Times again print all the news that fits?" Mr. Correra was a master mocker and, at the same time, a stickler for the plain truth. He had no truck with euphemism, loose metaphor, ambiguous analogy, glittering generality, or other journalistic crimes and misdemeanors. He was especially tough on unsubstantiated sources. Mr. Correra called all this civics. But this was not an instance of plain talk. Mr. Correra really taught epistemology.

Madame Morin was a romantic. She taught French. She

was French. And she pronounced and insisted we pronounce Morin like meringue but with an almost imperceptible Gallic difference that did not seem important to me till she explained one day that her antipathy for meringue was derived from the circumstance that meringue was derived from the German *Mehringen*. Which reenforced my dawning appreciation of the importance of the seemingly small, especially of seemingly small matters invested with boundless emotion.

Madame Morin taught many things. After we had learned each day to say, "Bonjour Madame Morin," Madame Morin would ask each day, "Quel est le jour?" Consequently, though I never learned to say Morin quite rightly, I can say "C'est aujoud hui Lundi" with considerable facility, and I am still pretty good on "mille neuf cent trente neuf," although I'm a bit slow on naming the years that have come since. In any case, what I learned especially from Madame Morin is less a consequence of the happenings at the beginning of each class than of those at the closing. Madame Morin would mark the penultimate moments by playing a recording of the Marseillaise. And we would mark that playing of the Marseillaise by standing up and singing. To which, Madame Morin would respond by crying. Always. Toujours. Which crying had nothing to do with the quality of our singing. Rien. Mille neuf cent trente neuf was the year the Nazis had overrun her beloved France. And to this day, I cannot hear the Marseillaise without tears welling up, and I cannot see the cabaret scene in Casablanca without breaking up. But Madame Morin taught me more than welling and breaking. As a result of her heartfelt teaching, I have a lasting affection for the French. Which has helped me frequently to get on passably in France despite a woeful lack of proficiency in the language Madame Morin tried to teach so heroically. Moreover, I can say most assuredly that what Madame Morin taught me most touchingly is how much can be conveyed by a few mumbled words if accompanied by the right gestures. Many teachers can teach French. Some may teach it better than Madame Morin. But I doubt very much that many can match Madame Morin when it comes to teaching le beau geste.

At Cornell University, Professor Jenkins taught histology.

For nearly a year he had me looking at little pieces of tissue on little pieces of glass. And though I learned little about those little pieces of tissue, I learned that sometimes you can tell more about a little tissue by looking at it under high power, sometimes under medium, sometimes under low, and sometimes with the naked eye. Which may seem something of a comedown from all that I had learned in grammar and secondary school but it did teach me unforgettably that high tech is not always what it's cracked up to be. And it taught me the related and still larger truth that sometimes it pays to look at things carefully and sometimes to look at them carelessly. Which lesson stayed with me steadfastly long after I forgot everything else I was ostensibly learning about histology by looking so carefully at those little pieces of tissue.

Professor Thompson taught Professor Thompson. Professor Thompson was short and heavy-set with a bald pate and small eyes set behind very large and strong spectacles. Professor Thompson looked like an owl. But he was really a star. Professor Thompson—we always called him Prof. T.—would get up on the stage before the assembled multitude, never less than a few hundred, and in his baritone-bass would trip swiftly from a resonant "Boomalay boomalay boomalay boom" to a squeaky "I'm nobody. Who are you? Are You nobody too?" to "I went to the woods because I wished to live deliberately" to "We have the moon; let us not ask for the stars" and more poetry that has long since faded irretrievably. I have a limited grasp of American literature, but I learned from Prof. T.'s quixotic selectings and leapings that what sounds disjointed is always jointed, particularly if it comes from the heart; I also learned that what is said aloud is never the same as what is only in the mind's eye or ear. And those were among my best lessons in free association. What's more, I learned that if you listened very attentively to Prof. T.'s loftiest elevations they proved clear revelations of what would appear later on the examinations. Which gave me extensive practice in guessing what people are thinking but not saying; and that proved another highly significant contribution to the practice of my future occupation.

Nor was that all I learned from Prof. T.'s teaching of

American literature. I learned that in Prof. T.'s class everybody was a nobody, and somehow that made everybody a somebody, and that by speaking so movingly to himself, and seemingly never to any of us, Prof. T. spoke movingly to all, or almost all, of us. Which helped me to see what Emerson was saying. Which helped me also to see how silly it would be to expect a Prof. T. to teach the way Mr. Sales taught.

Mr. Sales taught elementary writing. Which was aptly named because our writing was never anything but elementary. And Mr. Sales had his own way of stressing the elementary. He would come right up close to an errant student and say loudly, "Be simple. Be simple. Be simple." To this day, I don't know why Mr. Sales preferred, "Be simple. Be simple. Be simple" to Thoreau's "Simplify. Simplify. Simplify." Unless Mr. Sales thought his version simpler. Nor could I ever figure out why Mr. Sales always said "Be simple" three times. I thought it would be simpler to say it once.

And sometimes, for reasons unclear, Mr. Sales would say, "Eschew elaborate embellishments. Eschew elaborate embellishments. Eschew elaborate embellishments." Moreover, after those triple injunctions, he would bare his larger than average teeth in something between a smile and a grimace—I personally thought it nearer a grimace—and it was never clear whether he bared his teeth to convey the elementary nature of his assertions, to suggest the presence of a tool for pruning the extraneous, or to threaten anyone foolish enough to ignore his exhortations. And though I never did learn to "Be simple. Be simple. Be simple.", or even to "Eschew elaborate embellishments. Eschew elaborate embellishments. Eschew elaborate embellishments," I did learn from Mr. Sales's teaching in elementary writing the importance of seeking the impossible, of finding it impossible, and of bearing the pain of that finding. Which may have been the best lesson I ever received about this basic requisite of both learning and teaching.

After other similarly liberal education, and after a considerably less liberal medical education about which the less said the better, the medical chief resident during my internship taught me my best lesson in timing. In those days we worked for forty eight hours and then were off for twenty four. Occasionally during the forty eight we would stretch out for a few moments to watch television in a little space called the intern's room. I don't know why it was called the intern's room; we were never there long enough to gain a sense of possession. And one reason we were never there long was that our chief resident, affectionately known as Chief, had a knack of barging in during those brief efforts at rest and recreation and of saying, "Work hard fellows. If you work hard, you get to be a resident." But though I never did learn to work well enough or hard enough between the hours twenty four to forty eight, and often not even in the hours zero to twenty four, I did learn inescapably from the Chief the utter futility of handing out excellent advice at precisely the wrong moment.

Nor did this dizzying pace of learning falter when I went on to other postgraduate education. When I was a beginning student of psychoanalysis, one of our teachers asserted that after the first hour of an analysis, the analyst should be able to predict the entire course and outcome of the analysis to come. This teacher was not the sort with whom even the friskiest students were inclined (openly) to argue. Any student could see what the outcome of such argument would be. But after that class—and after many of that teacher's classes—many students were inspired, as we might otherwise not have been, to retire to a nearby delicatessen and to consider at great length the hazards of self-fulfilling prophesy. Which, if not the best, is not the worst lesson I ever received in psychoanalysis. Moreover, years later I received a valuable follow-up lesson. I learned that this teacher had given up psychoanalysis and was practicing hypnosis. Which made me realize how fortunate it was that near that school where I first studied psychoanalysis, and near so many schools, there are so many delicatessens.

The conclusion to be drawn from my student days may be obvious. But a true teacher never shrinks from stating the obvious. My own teachers, looking forward, thought they were teaching me one thing; and I, looking back, have incontrovertible evidence they were over and over teaching another. That being the case, though in my own teaching I am certain I have been teaching in accord with students' hidden questions, and though I have felt and cautiously expressed enthusiasm for the benefits of that enterprise, I must admit I lack hard evidence—or even persuasive soft—that I have been doing what I think I have, or, if I have, that my enthusiasm is warranted. If it's true that my teachers did not know what they were teaching, it's true that I do not know what I have been teaching. That is, I know what I have been teaching; it's only that I have so little notion what my students have been learning.

Other Thoughts on Assessing Teaching

Some authorities say the answer to assessing teaching lies in assessing what our students are learning; and some say the answer to assessing that learning lies in testing. Most teachers, however, find testing exceedingly confusing.

Consider our dilemma. To count what our students learn, we have tests that count precisely; but, unfortunately, those tests count the trivial. We also have tests that count the pivotal; but, unfortunately, their count is unreliable. Faced accordingly with a Hobson's choice between counting the trivial precisely and the pivotal unreliably, the true teacher struggles valiantly, if vainly, to count and be counted.

Our problems in assessing don't lie solely in the deficiencies of our tests. Taking the measure of any method of teaching by any means whatsoever is bound to be baffling since every teacher toils in, relies on, benefits from, and is often perplexed by a promiscuous success.

The best hitters in baseball hit safely three times out of ten. Suppose, however, the conditions were such that the poorest hitters hit safely nine times out of ten. With differences so slight between the best and the worst, how could anyone say convincingly who was doing well and who was not?

One of the most prominent factors contributing to our promiscuous success, and so to our difficulties assessing, is the abiding tendency of ignorance toward spontaneous remission. That tendency, some call it the tendency of students to learn, places teachers in a position akin to that of physicians, whose treatments of disease are so often bettered by the many remissions that leave so many physicians beset by so many illusions about the efficacy of their many pills. To complicate matters still more, in teaching, as in doctoring, in the fight against ignorance as in the fight against disease, the practitioner's contagious enthusiasm for his or her preferred aims and means exerts its own powerfully propitious effects.

Our troubles don't stop there. Scatter any students in any school to study any subjects by any means, and those students, with few exceptions, will come out knowing more about many things than they did when they came in; and we happy but befuddled teachers will never know whether that learning was a response to our teaching, to another teacher's teaching, to our students teaching themselves or each other, or to extracurricular or extraschool events, or to all of the above and more. Nor are our efforts at assessing made easier by the common happening that learning proceeds slowly and nearly imperceptibly in one area and surfaces abruptly and accelerates unaccountably in another. Which means one teacher is highly likely to get too little credit, and another is just as likely to get too much.

We teach more than we think. We teach less. We think we teach one thing. We teach another. We think we teach one way. We teach another. And even when we seem to have managed to teach what we have wanted to teach, we do not know how we have managed to teach it or how our students have managed to learn it.

We try to teach someone to swim. That person may learn.

But we cannot follow, and never shall, the endless subtleties and vagaries of ideas, sensations, feelings, and actions by which the swimming has begun to be learned. And even if we know a few paltry particulars we hope to teach, and have managed to teach a few, we can never hope to know how the novice natator has bridged between those paltry particulars and the substantial wisdom that adds up at last to swimming.

In all our confusion about what works best and what works worst, one thing remains clear. The best schools are schools attended by the best students; and the best students are attracted to the schools attended by the best students. And so if we look to those schools with a reputation for being best, we cannot determine how much of that reputation for excellence is a consequence of the excellence of the schools or of the students attracted by those schools, since the best students tend to do well even if the teaching to which they are subjected is not the best and is often the worst. Therefore it's impossible to fathom if the philosophies and methods of those teachers in the best schools account in large or small part for the success of the students or if that success is mainly the consequence of the packing together—the density, so to speak—of bright students who insist on learning, and have the knack of learning, in ways largely independent of the curricula, methods, philosophies, and other quirks of even their most dedicated, most spirited, and best-intended teachers.

What's more, many students do well in all sorts of schools not merely in spite of the worst teaching but because of it. This antithetical effect is a highly potent though insufficiently acknowledged determinant of many teaching successes. And the potency, frequency, and ubiquity of that antithetical effect suggests it may be a specialized instance of the general circumstance that in human events the best consequences often arise from the most poorly conceived acts carried out in the most poorly conceived manner for the most poorly conceived, and even the most reprehensible, purposes.

A large component of this salutary antithetical effect in teaching comes of our providing our students with conspicuously good examples of how not to proceed. And the true teacher, despite the widespread misconception that a teacher should set a good example, is always ready, willing, and able to set a sufficiently bad.

But we are confronted by the trickiest problems in assessing learning and teaching when we teach students who are especially adept at learning to do as we do or at least at learning to do what we tell them we do. And though we know abstractly and can bemoan fittingly that those who learn to talk like parrots will never learn to sing like larks, we find our students' imitations of ourselves, if not the sincerest form of flattery, among the most persuasive. Consequently, many students, having learned the fine art of academic mime in many schools over many years—without which they might never have gotten the credits necessary to join our present company—are then, upon finding us so inclined to see imitation as indicative of the excellence of our teaching and of our students' learning, encouraged irresistibly to practice and advance that art.

Those who are not teachers might find it hard to grasp why we teachers are so gullible. Their ignorance is understandable because they probably don't know what it's like to move so often in the classroom like Gulliver among the Lilliputians and to move so often outside the classroom like Gulliver among the Brobdingnagians; which terrible turn at the end of each day from the teaching world to the real is enough to give any teacher the bends; which heightens immeasurably our classroom vulnerability to flattery, our willingness to embrace the slightest signs that our teaching has made its mark, and our urgency to tell of the excellent consequences of teaching in the ways we prefer, or are compelled, to teach.

Nevertheless, though it's very hard to work in circumstances in which it's very hard to gain a clear view of the worth of one's work, I take considerable comfort from what one of my teachers told me one of his teachers told him. That teacher of my teacher said that on meeting his former students long after he had taught them, he had often been distressed to find that the students he thought he had taught the most seemed often to have learned the least. And the students he thought he had taught the least, seemed often to have learned the most. And some whom he had thought he had taught one thing seemed often to have learned another. Moreover, students often praised him for having taught what he could not recall having taught; and some praised him for having taught what he found most embarrassing to contemplate having taught. Still, having considered the matter for many years, he had concluded that any teacher who needs urgently to know whether and how his or her teaching has been useful is decidedly in the wrong line of work.